"Building off an extraordinary career where he worked effectively with stakeholders and elected officials, Steve shares gifts of knowledge that can help anyone be a stronger public service leader."

—Peter DeFazio, former chair of the US House Transportation and Infrastructure Committee

"Steve Wright is a proven leader who understands trust is where the magic happens. It's foundational to building the strong relationships necessary to find success and deliver results in today's world. His thoughtful approach to leadership is sure to inspire and motivate readers across the political spectrum."

—Cathy McMorris Rodgers, US Representative, chair of House Energy and Commerce Committee

"To those who believe each of us has the opportunity to create positive and meaningful change in the world through public service, Steve Wright has provided you the tools to help make it happen. I have worked with Steve, and I know he lives what he writes."

—Former Washington State governor, Christine Gregoire

"Steve Wright's career demonstrates that public service is indeed a noble calling. Inspired Public Service charts the path for the next generation to effectively lead the government and ensure the public interest is always top of mind."

—Rich Glick, former chairman, Federal Energy Regulatory Commission

"I worked very closely with Steve Wright during my six years at the US Department of Energy. Not only did Steve have my absolute trust and respect, I saw firsthand that he also had the trust and respect of cabinet officials, US senators, members of Congress, and both political and career officials throughout the federal government. That respect was earned. Rarely have I ever worked with anyone who was as effective as Steve in managing a large government organization, while also effectively working with members of both political parties. Steve's lessons on how to do on this are useful to anyone interested in how government can and should function."

—David Hill, former US Department of Energy General Counsel

"Throughout his years with the Bonneville Power Administration, Steve Wright was the embodiment of a "public servant." He was always willing to work with anyone—utilities, members of the public, elected officials of both parties, federal, state, and local community leaders—in the pursuit of goals that would serve the public interest. His lessons on how to do that are important for anyone interested in the effective functioning of American government."

—Scott Corwin, CEO of the American Public Power Association

"Having served as a CEO for nearly three decades, I've encountered numerous leadership philosophies and styles. Yet, having Steve as an executive coach has been a standout experience. His unique blend of purpose-focused leadership and a career dedicated to public service has provided me with invaluable insights and guidance. I know I'm a better leader because of Steve's counseling. This book is a testament to the profound impact that principled public service can have on effective leadership."

—Mike Peters, CEO WPPI Energy

"Steve led our public power agency's strategic planning with great skill, wisdom, and insight, defining KPP Energy's course for the next four years. In my 30+ years of work in public power, I've yet to participate in a strategic planning retreat that I felt was more organized, thoughtful, and inclusive. His deep knowledge of the utility industry—and of organizational leadership, management, and board governance—was invaluable to our agency."

—Colin Hansen, CEO, KPP Energy

"I've had the privilege and pleasure of working with Steve in a variety of roles—as a peer, as a fellow board member for our national trade organization, and most recently in his role as a strategic planning consultant for AMP. Steve has deep industry knowledge and the finesse to effectively engage a broad range of people. I'm very pleased with Steve's work with AMP and our board of trustees."

—Jolene Thompson, CEO, American Municipal Power

INSPIRED PUBLIC SERVICE

Cover photo: Bonneville Power Administration

Book design and publishing management: Bryan Tomasovich

Wright, Steve
Inspired Public Service: A Guide to Building Pride, Purpose, and Democracy

ISBN: 979-8-218-37977-3

1. Political Science / Public Affairs and Administration
2. Business & Economics / Leadership.
3. Political Science / Public Policy
4. Political Science / American Government

Distributed by Ingram

Printed in the United States of America

INSPIRED PUBLIC SERVICE

A Guide to Building Pride, Purpose, and Democracy

STEVE WRIGHT

*I*NSPIRED PUBLIC SERVICE

To Kathleen

Thanks for your kindness and patience

To be loved makes all things seem possible

INTRODUCTION

The first thing we could hear were the buses. There were quite a few of them pulling to a stop, then idling out of sight. And then the voices, seeking to be heard over a long distance, gathering strength, moving closer to our building. Then we began to see the people, many of them wearing gray T-shirts with letters emblazoned on the front. Their chants reflected the T-shirts: *Wright is Wrong* they shouted, as they gathered in the courtyard below my office window.

We had known they were coming, but we didn't expect the group to be as large as it was. Roughly four hundred people milled around, demanding that I come down to speak with them. Some were less than kind with their shouted comments about my intestinal fortitude to come face-to-face with them. They were aluminum workers and their families. Many of them angry, borne from the fear that they would lose their jobs, and their communities would be devastated—due to decisions I had proposed to make.

Television crews had set up, no doubt having been tipped off in advance. Our security people were not excited about me going into the middle of the crowd. There was no realistic way to protect me. Yet, our public relations people noted the obvious: to not go down into the crowd would have symbolic repercussions of an isolated federal agency uncaring about its impact on the people it was created to serve.

I felt I had no choice but to accommodate the crowd's requests. I was a public servant. I had committed long ago to a career of serving the public interest. These were people who had the right to petition their government. So, I went down, waded into the middle of the tightly packed crowd. My heart was racing. There was a modest physical threat, but to me the greater concern was whether I would reach or lose their hearts and minds. I stood up and did my best to explain what we were trying to accomplish, why and how we were attempting to protect their interests. I fielded questions yelled at me along the way, all the while feeling the pulse of the crowd rising and falling on my every sentence.

This was one of many times when I found that, despite thinking I was prepared after many years of training, I still had a lot to learn as a leader in the public sector. I had a graduate degree in public administration and had spent twenty years surrounded by the leaders of my agency. I was months into assuming the reigns of leadership, yet frequently realizing I had a lot of blind spots in my approach. I spent the next twenty years in leadership positions—in large public sector organizations, federal and local government, and not-for-profit organizations—constantly discovering better ways to lead that would help my organizations be more successful.

In this book, I share the most important learning I have experienced along my journey in public sector leadership. My goal is to help others accelerate their learning curve and (hopefully) not make as many false starts or outright mistakes that I have made.

Working in public service was a conscious decision for me. I *had* intended to be a sportswriter, and then a psychologist, and ended up with undergraduate majors in both. But along the way, I had taken the opportunity to engage in some state legislative processes, and then some political campaigns. I loved the idea of engaging in public policy choices to try to make the world a better place. Hence, I chose to go to graduate school, focusing on public administration, a choice that led me fortuitously to the University of Oregon.

On the day of Ronald Reagan's inauguration in 1981, I was hired for an entry-level position by the Bonneville Power Administration (BPA). BPA is a federal agency, part of the US Department of Energy, with responsibilities to provide transmission and market electricity from the federal hydropower projects in the Pacific Northwest, including such venerable structures as the Grand Coulee and Bonneville Dams.

The symmetry to being hired on President Reagan's first day in office has always been important to me. I have great respect for President Reagan, but on one point I felt he encouraged what has become an enduring problem: he uttered the often-repeated phrase, "Government is the problem, not the solution."

In many respects, President Reagan was only highlighting what a broad sector of society was thinking. The President's statement was fundamentally about the need to reduce the *size* of government. But, it also pointed to a growing sense of government failure; unfortunately, that has translated into a lack of respect for people who choose a career in government service. This is both unfair and a challenge to those who choose to dedicate their careers to public service—and seek to counter this misperception.

My view is not that government is always good. Government can make mistakes and create problems. Government can get too big and spend too much. But government can, and frequently does, add value to achieve the public's objectives. Even in an intensely capitalistic society, government is necessary to establish rule of law to assure citizens can fairly reap the rewards of their efforts. The challenge is to think broadly about what best serves the public interest, then utilizing governmental tools in the right ways to add value for the common good.

In November 2000, I became the BPA Administrator/CEO. Candidly, I moved into this role with much policy making and little management experience. Predictably, I was better at what I was experienced at.

Picked originally by the Clinton Administration to serve in an acting capacity, I was selected by the Bush Administration for the permanent role with the bipartisan support of the Northwest Senate delegation (including the four Democratic and four Republican senators from Montana, Idaho, Oregon, and Washington), and then asked to stay on by President Obama's administration in 2009, after again receiving unanimous bipartisan support. I take great pride in gaining and maintaining bipartisan support for over a decade in a controversial political environment.

BPA has over three thousand employees with annual revenues and expenditures in the range of $3.5 billion. It's a relatively large stage to play upon, and I spent a great deal of time in the public spotlight. I led the agency through the west coast energy crisis, debates about the extent energy efficiency should be relied upon, the impact of the federal hydropower system on endangered salmon, the development of new transmission for reliability, expanding access to the grid for wind power, and how a federal electric power marketing agency should participate in competitive markets. I got some decisions right, and some wrong—although there is some debate about which fit in the two categories.

From there I spent eight years leading the Chelan County, Washington Public Utility District, a consumer-owned electric, water, wastewater, and fiber business in north central Washington. There I got the opportunity to practice what I had learned, and grow further. While still in the public sector, I was now outside the federal government. Chelan did not have the high-level political challenges that I encountered at the BPA, but the issues still involved how to balance the needs for a clean, affordable, and reliable power system. I also got to see the effects of our decisions more closely on the public, because it was providing service at the retail level. While the reach was not as big as BPA, the lessons were just as powerful because of being accessible daily to the citizens we served.

While at Chelan, I was able to serve on multiple boards, including for the Alliance to Save Energy, an organization that leads Washington, DC policymaking supporting energy efficiency, and a trade group, the American Public Power Association.

This book is not a story about the controversies associated with those jobs, however, or my role in them. I share this background just to say that my experience leading in the public sector ranges from difficult, highly visible policy and overtly political circumstances to managing operations, personnel, finances, budgets, and legal strategies. From a national and regional stage, to local issues. Ultimately, the lessons shared here are more universal to public service than a focus on electricity policy.

While this book touches on how to perform good public policy analysis, the focus is on public administration: how to create management structure and culture that leads to high-quality public policy decision-making, and sound public policy. This is not an academic treatise backed by rigorous analytical data. This is simply a report on my experiential learning. When describing something as effective, I simply mean it worked for me.

My challenge to readers is to strive for performance improvement in the government sector that is measured by the satisfaction of the people we serve. My aim is to describe actions government leaders can take to build a culture that will lead to improvements in effectiveness and efficiency, and thereby improve the public's attitude about government and the work of public servants. It is imperative to improve trust in government, as it is a necessary component to preserving our democracy.

INTRODUCTION

I often refer to tools commonly applied in the private sector, but tailor them in a manner that will contribute to success in the public sector. There are also tools that are unique to government. With a couple of exceptions, I did not invent these tools. I learned from others inside and outside of government, more by osmosis than personal revelation.

I also disagree with the conventional wisdom that bipartisanship is dead, but that said, the pursuit of bipartisan solutions should not be left up to incredibly overloaded elected officials alone. There are actions public-sector employees can take that promote the adoption of bipartisan solutions.

The leadership practices I describe from my career led to high satisfaction scores by key constituencies—the primary measure of a public agency's success. They also garnered broad bipartisan support for the agency, despite serving an extraordinarily diverse set of stakeholders that spanned the political spectrum.

The simple, yet incredibly powerful concept of driving all strategy and decisions through an articulated commitment to serving the public interest is the north star that I returned to over and over when leading BPA and Chelan. It's the fundamental magic elixir providing the foundation for success, readily available though underutilized at most government agencies. . .

This simple tool, rigorously and effectively applied, generates pride, leads to continuous improvement, and breaks down silos within and across governmental organizations. When successfully applied, it can help change for the better the public's perception of public servants and public service careers.

The ideas described in this book were generated from a variety of people over decades of discussions at BPA and at Chelan. I do not mean to take credit for them simply because I have authored the book. I believe the concepts described here brought structure and rigor that allowed BPA and Chelan to be viewed as successful by a wide array, although not all, stakeholders, and political actors.

I want to be clear that I did not always meet my own standards that I lay out here. I would lose my compass, get immersed in details, and forget the bigger picture of the objective of serving the public interest. Many of the actions described here were things I learned along the way from making mistakes. The tools described here would help me regain my footing and reorient toward the north star of the meaning behind public service. For me, it was always a process of continuous improvement, and that journey has not come to an end.

During my career in leadership, I learned there is power unleashed by the simple thought of focusing on serving the public interest. I held hundreds of employee meetings: it's easy to feel when the audience is engaged with you, and when it is not. Bringing the conversation back to the basics of serving the public interest, relating the principle to the issue at hand, increased employee engagement. It is motivating and energizing for most employees. It drives behavior that is based on meeting the needs of the public, rather than personal or individual objectives, which brings greater meaning and purpose to life.

I didn't write this book because I believe I have finally reached the *nirvana* of understanding how to best serve the public interest. But, I learned along the way how powerfully that phrase, used sincerely and repeatedly, can lead to better outcomes. How it energizes employees and centers decision-making. How it connects with the public, creating a valuable window into the decision-making processes. I was better at understanding how to employ it by the time I finished than when I started. I could have done better earlier in my career if I had been more aware of the tools shared in this book.

While this book focuses on the potential impacts of building an agency strategy around serving the public interest, the benefits goes beyond what can be accomplished at work. A focus on public service brought meaning and purpose to my life. It caused me to strive to make the world a better place outside of my work responsibilities.

Because it is based on my experience, this book focuses on leaders and potential leaders operating in the executive branch of federal, state, or local governments. But implicit in this discussion are also lessons for legislative branch employees, as well as not-for-profit and non-governmental organizations. Some private sector businesses, particularly those that are engaged in sectors that are heavily regulated, could also see benefit.

While the book is designed to create value no matter where a person is in their career, it speaks to leaders and those who want to lead. It provides lessons for people just starting, to those with vast experience who are looking to polish skills. For public administration students, it's a guide to consider public policy management as a necessary complement to public policy analysis. If you are new or mid-career in public service management, the book covers an array of management structures and skills that can be adopted as an integrated holistic approach, or as individual pieces. If you are an accomplished leader who recognizes some of the tools described, take a look at the conclusions at the end of each chapter to identify new tools for your management arsenal.

There are five parts in the book, each focused on an important piece of inspired public service: 1) how to use the power of public service as a motivational tool; 2)how to utilize serving the public interest as foundational to building a successful public service organization; 3) how to build public service into your agency culture; 4) how to create bipartisan solutions; and, 5) how to develop your leadership skills using public service values.

My hope is that those engaged in public service will find in this book actions that increase their effectiveness and the success of their organizations. Moreover, I want to contribute toward creating greater public confidence in government and the employees who serve. Most importantly, my goal is to strengthen the democracy we love.

So, how did the aluminum-worker protest turn out, described at the beginning of the chapter? The engagement, while tense, was remarkably positive. While there was some hostility shouted at me as I was approaching the crowd and during speaking, I stuck to an approach that is described in Chapters 12 and 13 about communications and giving speeches, particularly regarding speaking to the audience's hearts and minds. At that time, I don't think I could have articulated the principles I used, but over the years, they became increasingly clear to me. Those principles that work in countless situations are what I want to share.

There were moments that went well, and moments when I nearly lost the crowd. After finishing the formal back-and-forth discussion, I stepped down and was surrounded by people asking more questions. Another moment when our security folks were very uncomfortable. But amid those questions, I got one about how a specific action would impact the communities where the aluminum plants were located, an issue we had not considered. I had to pause because I knew they wanted an answer right then, and the temptation was to answer *yes*. But in truth, I did not know the consequences, so I committed to look into it. We did investigate and were able to improve our approach to the original plan.

I took away a lifelong lesson: engaging the public in a meaningful way, even under difficult conditions, can create value. Despite many hours of an organization's preparation, there are things that members of the public know about their circumstances that can and should influence public policy. And when their lives are being impacted, they deserve to be heard in a meaningful way.

Serving the public interest

How is the term "serving the public interest" used in this book? Let's take a moment to describe what is meant, and not.

This is not an academic exercise, reviewing historical ideas defining the public interest. I don't have the academic training to be qualified. Rather, my definition is illuminated by experience.

The public interest is a concept that is referred to in various ways: *the common good, common well-being, general welfare,* or *public benefit* are often synonyms for the public interest. All these terms speak to moving beyond individual or small-group self-interest to the well-being of a collective group.

We live in a society that holds as a foundation the philosophy of Adam Smith: that individuals acting in their self-interest will create greatest societal value. Certainly capitalist-based systems have produced great wealth and prosperity. Yet, this philosophy does not extend to a system of anarchy. Capitalist systems always include a role for government, to address actions that are unlikely to happen through self-interest alone. Instead, there is organized collective action that provides for the common good: national defense, infrastructure development, crime prevention, and environmental protection. The public interest defines where individuals acting in their self-interest should be left alone, versus where the need for collective action is necessary to promote the general welfare. Government is organized around pursuing strategies that support the common good that would not occur in its absence.

The public interest is dynamic, not static. It is constantly evolving as the views of the public change. Ultimately, the public interest is defined by how people vote. Democratically elected officials, as representatives of the people, provide the best source of divining the public interest. An individual committed to serving the public will not only hear directly from the public. They also work with elected officials who have the ultimate accountability, since they were elected to determine the public's interests and values. More on this in Chapters 10 and 11, where we will discuss how agency officials can partner with elected officials to best define the public interest.

INTRODUCTION

So, the public interest starts from a basis of creating good for the benefit of the public that would not otherwise occur. Individuals or organizations pursuing their self-interest while part of a public sector organization are the antithesis of serving the public interest. In fact, we view these as ethical violations that are subject to discipline and ridicule.

I hope you will find insights in this book that lead you to more fulfillment and success. More importantly, I hope in some small way it helps improve the performance of government, all toward strengthening the pillars of democracy through inspired public service.

Each of the chapters of this book initiates with an inspirational quote about public service. To start you off on your journey to inspired public service, here is my favorite quote:

"It is not the critic who counts, not the man who points out how the strong man stumbled, or where the doer of deeds could have done better. The credit belongs to the man who is actually in the arena, whose face is marred by dust and sweat and blood, who strives valiantly, who errs and comes up short again and again, who knows the great enthusiasms, the great devotions, and spends himself in a worthy cause, who at best knows the achievement and at the worst if he fails at least fails while daring greatly so that his place shall never be with those cold and timid souls who know neither victory nor defeat."

—Theodore Roosevelt

PART 1

Building Purpose, Pride, Bipartisanship, and Democracy

1

Cultivating Inspired Public Service

What counts in life is not the mere fact we have lived. It is what difference we have made to the lives of others that will determine the significance of the life we lead.

—Nelson Mandela

Picture a public meeting where there is a long line of people waiting for their opportunity to make their comments heard. A woman and her two small children come forward to the microphone. She hesitatingly and politely describes that her husband, who works in the industry, is the primary breadwinner in their family, and he is at risk of losing his job. The main issue of the meeting pertains to how costs and benefits will be allocated, and there is a particular sense of urgency because a group of industrial customers are facing global competitive challenges, threatening their continued operation.

Yet, this woman brought a different point of view of the industry. I've seen the statistics. I know when the primary breadwinner is out of work, the risk of alcohol abuse and domestic violence increases. I don't know if that will affect her family, but I know if her husband loses his job, their odds get worse.

Finally she said, "We didn't do anything wrong. We were just living our lives. The actions of your agency are what is putting my family at risk. Do something. Make it stop. Let us get back to living our lives."

It was a powerful moment for me. I had always wanted to be in a position of being able to make a meaningful difference in other people's lives. But the weight of that responsibility got a lot heavier in that moment. I could argue with her that it wasn't all our fault, but she was right that at least some of the solution lay in our hands.

KEY TAKEAWAYS

The erosion of public trust in government and its employees is a fundamental threat to democracy. There is a compelling need to overcome the dominant negative perceptions of government and its employees.

Civil service leaders can help alter the trend. We have the opportunity—not to be victims—but to take affirmative action to restore the luster of government and government service.

This is not easy work. Solving for serving the public interest is harder due to multiple variables, than solving for profit alone.

Establish an inspired public service culture focused on embracing the strength of finding meaning and purpose through work. The value created by public sector work is a key strength that generates commitment to a cause.

Public service leaders can motivate through articulating how the organization's tasks lead to improving quality of life for employees' relatives, friends, neighbors, and community.

The way a leader shows up in the workplace impacts the extent to which a public service culture is established. They must demonstrate that public service is a noble cause.

Beyond sincerity, a leader must integrate serving the public interest through a systemic approach, using tools such as mission, vision, values, strategic plans, and performance plans. When included in these aspects of organizational culture, the reach of the leader is expanded.

Building culture and strategy around serving the public interest can:
- Provide strategic clarity, increasing efficiency and effectiveness
- Lead to more durable outcomes
- Cause employees to take ownership and seek continuous improvement
- Lead to greater public support and build potential bipartisanship
- Produce greater public satisfaction and elected official support
- Build respect, enhancing recruiting and retention
- Elevate public confidence, thereby strengthening democracy

Democracy is in peril

Our country, our democracy, is on a dangerous path. The American public's confidence in its government has been eroding for decades. It has been a slow but steady decline. But the proverbial frog in the pot is getting boiled.

Pew Research has polled the same question for over sixty years with dismaying results. The percentage of Americans who trust the government in Washington, DC always or most of the time has fallen from the 70-80% range in the 1950s/early 1960s to the 20 percent range in 2010-2020.

This is not a small problem for a government defined by Abraham Lincoln as, "of the people, by the people, for the people." A belief that government is not serving the people is so at odds with government *for the people* that it suggests a need for radical change.

Democracy, for all its warts, remains the best alternative to any other form of government. A healthy skepticism of government and the people who choose to work there can be grounds for constructive policy debate. But blatant disdain for government and dismissal of the people who are attempting to accomplish the role of government undermines our democratic institutions.

We can debate how much government we need, but at whatever level it operates, we need effective government for fundamental necessities like a strong economy, national security, and a healthy environment. When trust is broken and lost, it becomes difficult for any government, but especially a democratic government, to perform its basic functions. The lack of effective democratic government is a pathway to anarchy— or, in response to chaos, totalitarianism.

Altering the path

As big as this problem is with our confidence in government, there are important contributions that can be made from inside government that can help restore it. We can be part of the solution. It should be our goal to turn this trend around. As leaders and potential leaders in government, we may not have total control over this perilous slide. But that's not a valid excuse for inaction.

This is a call for improving the performance of government in a way the public we are charged with serving will recognize and applaud. Yet, to be clear, it's certainly not a polemic for ever greater roles for government. We should have the government we need to promote the common welfare—and no more.

As leaders in public service, we can blame the people we serve for not understanding the importance of our work. We can blame elected officials for the increasing partisanship, along with the lack of respect for government workers.

Or, we can choose not to be victims. We can lay out a positive agenda that is built around meeting the public's needs, as they define it, as its core agenda. We can take action that seeks to change the widespread negative views of the government and its workers. Changing this paradigm can only occur based on a thoughtful plan, faithfully implemented brick by brick, by a cadre of committed public servants who are devoted to the value to our democratic institutions of rebuilding public trust in their government.

Government service should be held in high regard as a career choice. It is easy to envision what we would want to enrich our lives and careers: a widespread belief that government exists to serve the greater good of the community.

Overcoming the dominant perceptions

What would be expected from a child who grew up in a world that delivered these messages to them on a regular basis? *Your efforts are inferior and even the products you manage to produce are unnecessary. Your work habits are slovenly. You could not survive if you had to compete against your peers. You should consider yourself fortunate that the rest of us carry your deadweight. In short, you are incompetent and inferior.*

Likely, we would be concerned about the effects of this kind of verbal abuse on a child's self-esteem and development. If this form of abuse was directed at a class of people, we would view it as discrimination.

Yet, this is the world in which public servants are immersed. We live in a culture that deems it acceptable to malign public service and public servants. The culture around us bombards us with expectations of failure. It is so pervasive that it colors the perspective of even those of us who affirmatively choose public service as a career.

After being criticized for so long in an all-encompassing environment, there is a form of Stockholm syndrome within public sector employees. There is a tendency to choose not to argue, but rather to agree with their critics, even maligning their own work. They, too, become cynics about the potential for government to succeed.

"A workforce focused on public service improves outcomes and provides hope for turning around the lack of trust in government."

I've seen this in myself: Nodding my head knowingly as someone complains about how government can't get anything right, while internally feeling the dissonance associated with thinking that they, unwittingly, are speaking about *me*, because I'm a government employee.

It's easy to become cynical and detached as a public sector employee. It's a normal human reaction to sustained criticism, coming from many directions: media that focus primarily on programs and policies that do not match expectations, yet avoid reporting on things that go right. Elected officials that harp on the negatives of government. Even our friends, neighbors, and relatives who express disdain for government "bureaucrats."

It's challenging to reject the cynicism about government and government employees that surrounds us, while setting the performance standards high. Yet, we know there are many smart, hard-working people in government. Many who intrinsically connect with providing public service. People who enjoy working on issues that are important and make a difference. People who love to be challenged. There are many people who have left government who say they miss the relevance and importance of the work they did. Our goal should be to pull more employees toward the light of opportunity, and away from cynicism.

The mission is hard

Even with high levels of motivation, public service is extraordinarily difficult work.

When solving for the public interest, you're not working with an easy, clear goal line like profit or loss. Serving the public interest means addressing a problem that is comprised of multiple variables such as the economy, the environment, national security, etc. Given these challenges, public service requires indefatigable commitment in order to succeed. It requires getting all your people on the same page, with focused attention on what needs to get done, and how to get it done with collaboration and quality.

Connecting to meaning and purpose

Inspired public service is about establishing a culture built on providing meaning and purpose through service to others. The most important actions we take as leaders are not the substantive policy and program decisions. What has the deepest impact is the culture we establish in our organizations. The culture is determined by defining what represents high quality work processes and decisions. Get this right and in most cases the result will be good substantive policy and program decisions.

We know that to achieve great outcomes people must be highly motivated. Finding meaning and purpose inspires employees by providing the "why" their work is important. It leads to a commitment to a cause. Commitment to a cause leads to extraordinary effort.

Moreover, increasing the focus on serving the public interest creates the energy to assume the difficult chores of public service. It helps turn around the inferiority complex experienced by many public sector employees through instilling pride. Instead, public servants strive for being great, because of the importance and need for their superior efforts.

Playing to our strength

Public service is a subject frequently treated as old-fashioned. Naïve. Idealistic to a fault. Or it's perceived as implicit. Calling it out as a virtue can seem perfunctory.

But while the idea may be old, the emotion it evokes remains fresh. The famous John F. Kennedy phrase, "Ask not what your country can do for you, but rather what you can do for your country," still evokes a positive emotional reaction. It does so because of the altruistic passion with which it was uttered.

Serving the public interest is what makes government different from the private sector because it starts from the altruistic perspective looking out for the common good, rather than individual self-interest. The importance of what we do in the public sector is our strength. We don't sell pet rocks in the public sector.

Great public sector leaders translate specific tasks of their organization into the grander vision of how the work leads to improving the quality of life for their fellow citizens. When that connection gets made, emotional commitment is cemented, creating the best avenue for employees to bring their heart and soul to their work. Emotional connection can be translated into actions and results. It is more relevant today as a motivational tool than ever before, as younger generations demand more meaning and purpose in their employment. Public service offers just that, so we need to play to our strengths.

Showing up with sincerity

To get the most out of a culture built around pride in public service, it's important to lead with passion and sincerity when demonstrating the value of your organization's work. Mouthing the words won't cut it. Speaking authentically about serving the public interest touches many people, inside and outside of government, in a manner that energizes and enhances credibility and respect.

Here are fundamental beliefs that build a foundation for a culture based on the power of pride in public service:

- Public service is a noble cause.
- Public service is altruistic because it is about choosing to focus on the interest of community, rather than self-interest. It is based on establishing as the highest priority, improving the quality of life for our fellow citizens. Therefore, there is honor and dignity in choosing public service.
- Inspired public servants hear and respect public input when seeking to improve the quality of life as the public defines it.
- Public service is essential to democracy, and must be performed superbly to preserve our democratic institutions.
- With the right spark and structure, government agencies can deliver services excellently and government employees can produce results at a superior level.
- Public confidence in government can be elevated.
- Bipartisanship may be wounded, but it is not dead. Efforts from outside the formal legislative processes by executive branch employees with unique expertise and collaboration skills to develop solutions can build a foundation for bipartisan support.
- Most elected officials are committed to public service and are best in touch with defining the constantly evolving definition of what best

serves the public interest. They are looking for partners who are committed to finding workable solutions that balance the desires of their constituents.

- Be unwilling to accept the simple solution that making decisions means making many people unhappy. Challenging, hard, and frustrating it may be, but doing something worthwhile, that truly makes the public happy, is not expected to be easy.

How do we make it systemic?

Sincerity, though, is not enough. There must be an organized system for employing the concepts of focusing on public service, such that they become embedded in driving everything from strategy to policy development to program implementation to day-to-day interactions with the public.

This book describes how the simple concept of serving the public interest can become the foundation of your culture through infusing it into your mission, vision and especially values. How it can then be translated into your strategic plan, performance objectives, and daily decision-making. How to create positive accountability rejecting the notion that the public sector produces inferior work to the private sector. How to use the public service ethic in your internal and external communications. How to instill a commitment to serve the public interest as a foundation to work with elected officials for durable solutions.

Why does building strategy around serving the public interest work?

It creates strategic clarity on how an agency's actions are impacting the public, improving efficiency and effectiveness. It's easy to get caught up in getting a goal accomplished and lose track of the impact on the people we serve. For example, at one point we were attempting to construct a much-needed substation necessary for keeping the lights on. There was opposition from nearby homeowners. Our organization began to think of the opponents as the enemy. We needed to do an internal reset that started with focusing on our mission, vision, and values. That led to recognizing the opponents were part of the public that we served. We needed to find ways to better work with all the public to best achieve the public interest. That led to the next outcome….

It encourages employees to strive to understand the public they serve, leading to more dialogue and collaboration that results in more durable outcomes. It breaks down internal silos through identifying the "north star" for agency activities. When we acknowledged these stakeholders as part of the public we were committed to serve, the dialogue changed. It moved us away from defeating them so we could advance the project toward how we might shift some of the total benefits to the greater public from building the project toward local stakeholders. This embraced a "no losers" philosophy, since the value to the common good was creating a cost for one group of stakeholders.

As we move toward regarding all of the public as people who we are working for, there is a greater openness to understanding critiques of our foundational data and materials. In this case, there was much local knowledge that helped to better inform our siting decisions. We needed to be open to hearing about all the relevant issues. That led to treating all members of the public as partners on the journey to serving the public interest. It also reduced the internal debates between the extreme edges of *just build it* versus concerns of individual commenters.

It can be deeply motivational for employees, and therefore deeply satisfying. It can create a greater sense of ownership in producing good outcomes, thereby leading to an internally generated drive for continuous improvement. A focus on getting the substation built in a timely way, but with substantial respect for and response to local concerns, helped to motivate employees. The goal became seeking a solution that met the electric reliability needs, while mitigating harm to local stakeholders. It placed our employees in a less antagonistic position with members of the public. Public service that is seeking to solve real world problems brings meaning and importance to work life. There is honor and dignity in focusing on the needs of others and seeking to create a better world.

Greater engagement and collaboration with the public in our processes can ultimately lead to greater support and bipartisanship in the legislative arena. Elected officials understand that controversy can create separation between political candidates. Controversy also creates an opportunity to go to bat for a constituent who believes they are not receiving due process from their government. On the other hand, my experience was that elected officials like to see progress being made where there are sincere efforts to reconcile various points of view. Elected officials are more willing to give explicit or tacit support to conclusions where there is a strong record that various points of view were engaged and faithfully sought to be addressed.

There was a strong recognition in the political arena that electric reliability was very important, and that a new substation was needed. But unhappy local constituents can create a need for elected officials to take their side, particularly when there is a sense that the constituents are not being heard. Steady efforts to serve all of the public—through engaging on all the issues the public raises, and seeking to treat everyone fairly—increases the odds of gaining bipartisan support.

It elevates public satisfaction and elected officials' confidence. That, in turn, leads to increased internal confidence. It can even aid recruiting and retention of the best and the brightest for government service. It builds respect for the institutions many of us have chosen to dedicate a significant portion of our lives. A deep and abiding leadership commitment to serving the public resonates through an agency and its outward persona. Solutions which show that different views have been heard and respected increase the likelihood of public support. That leads to increased internal confidence in agency competence. Prospective employees hear about an agency through its reputation, and an agency that is meeting the needs of the public will be an attractive place to work.

A dedicated focus on serving the public interest as the foremost goal of government can elevate the confidence in government and thereby strengthen our democracy. Ultimately, the public can tell whether the guidance from a public agency is coming from a place of either *try to work with them* or *roll over them.* A sincere attempt to find common ground with constituents establishes more fertile ground for respect of government. There is satisfaction in helping to strengthen our institutions built on the premise of the people being part of governing themselves.

Conclusion

This book will take you on a journey that turns the idealistic and esoteric into the practical. The goal is distant, difficult to envision, but worth striving for: an American public that appreciates its government and public servants because they have earned it through their commitment to serving the public interest.

What happened to the woman at the beginning of this chapter? I don't know for certain. I know we made considerable efforts to address our impact on her life and many others who were in similar situations. I have told and retold her story over the years as a means for bringing home that we as public servants have power to affect people's lives beyond what we may recognize. Our work is filled with meaning and purpose. Her story influenced my approach to governance by making the impact of our decisions real. It caused me to strive to find better solutions because the impact became more obvious.

It also caused me to want to lead in a manner that touched every employee with the relevance of their work to the lives of real people. Infusing the organization with the spirit of the importance of public service leads to a motivated workforce. A workforce focused on public service improves outcomes and provides hope for turning around the lack of trust in government. In this way, we can contribute to building a stronger foundation for democracy. May this book influence you to seek to be an inspired public servant.

2

The Power of Pride

If your actions inspire others to dream more, learn more, do more and become more, than you are a leader.

—John Quincy Adams

It's a bitter cold winter night. The aroma is pine trees and coffee. Portable floodlights illuminate the snow that is falling. Many trees are down as a result of a windstorm. Deenergized power lines are on the ground, too, many of the poles that previously supported them shattered. There is activity everywhere. The sound is primarily chainsaws. Linemen in hard hats and reflective vests are moving in earnest. New poles and wires are being put into position. People stare from inside their dark and cold homes, occasionally venturing out to ask what they can do to help. They are thanked, but asked to stay out of the way. This is a job for trained professionals who take great pride in knowing how to most efficiently get the electricity turned back on.

In the electric utility industry, public or private sector, there is no higher calling than keeping the lights on. There are a myriad of planning efforts designed to create high reliability. But no matter how much planning is done, circumstances arise when the lights go out. Most often, its due to weather events that cause most of us to want to stay inside. In those moments, we count on our linemen to venture out into inclement weather, with dangerous safety conditions, to restore service. It is an act of heroism exhibited on nearly a daily basis around the country.

Pride is an important tool available to government leaders to accentuate. Choosing to work in the public sector, just by its nature, means doing important and meaningful work. When done well, it creates the opportunity to improve the quality of life for people all around us. It's a gift public servants give to their fellow citizens. And like any gift, it can create joy for the giver.

KEY TAKEAWAYS

There is great motivational power associated with creating pride in public service. Yet it is mostly underutilized. We tend to shrink away from calling on it, because celebrating public service has become contrary to cultural norms.

We can unleash the power of pride that can be elicited with sincere repeated use of the phrase *serving the public interest*, backed up by systemic reinforcement.

It's up to public sector leaders to illuminate the connection between the work throughout the organization and its impact on real people. Connect the voices that you hear in public comment to your employees, so they can see how their work leads to meaningful outcomes.

Creating a strong connection between day-to-day work and serving the public interest supports a culture of continuous improvement, while enhancing recruitment and retention.

Creating a culture that focuses first on serving the public interest takes courage and sincerity on the part of a leader. It takes a willingness to consistently articulate a personal and organizational commitment to public service.

Controversy regarding policy objectives should be embraced and interpreted as evidence that your agency's work is meaningful to the public you serve. It's an opportunity to play an important role in defining how best to serve the public interest.

Encourage subject matter mastery by employees. It helps the public to make sound decisions based on best available data, while giving employees the opportunity to be great at something that is important to the communities you serve.

Using service to inspire

No doubt about it. We are fighting a battle. A battle to overcome the conventional wisdom in our society that tends to denigrate public service. A battle to overcome the cynicism that can surround us with the label of being "just another bureaucrat."

Confronted with a culture that frequently belittles public service, the path of least resistance can be to avoid the subject. This leads to underutilization of a *superpower*: service to others can be highly motivational. Repeated use of variations on the phrase—*we are here to serve the public interest*—provides meaning and purpose to work. It creates context and vision, helping to overcome the difficulties of day-to-day operations.

It's our job as leaders in the public sector to inspire our people with the understanding of the prodigious opportunities they have to make the world a better place. To create focus on the important responsibility that comes with serving the public interest.

It is our job to make the connections between work and outcomes that affect the public, creating a sense of pride, satisfaction, self-respect and a desire for continuous improvement. As pride grows so will organizational effectiveness. Pride is powerful, but too often latent in the government sector. The improvement in morale alone is enough reason to act. But even more, pride also causes people to strive for higher performance. It engages employees in improving processes and policies in order to better serve the public.

If you have worked in the public sector, you know there are high performers motivated by the importance of their work. Many public employees chose this profession because they were motivated by wanting to perform public service. For some, though, the original exhilaration may have eroded. They may need a motivational booster shot. Even those that chose the public sector because it was just a job they needed, they still have the potential to be motivated by the opportunity to do important work that improves the quality of life of their fellow citizens.

Create the connection

Working in large government agencies can divorce public servants from the reality of the impacts of their work on serving the public. The public may be invisible to the employee. They need to know how their work makes a meaningful and important difference.

"It is our job as public sector leaders to unleash the latent power of employee pride in public service."

They also need the reminder of the historical perspective of the great things the agency was created to perform to improve the quality of life. All agencies started with a high-minded vision for serving a pressing need—as defined by the public. We as leaders need to connect our people to both the history and the present higher calling that we serve.

As leaders we must extol the virtues of public service. To motivate through continually visualizing for your people the importance of their work. To tell the story. How many people's lives are impacted by the work we do? In what ways?

For example, for many agencies, their work supports the creation of jobs. When talking about job creation, go beyond telling the numbers story of how many jobs may be created by a particular program or policy. Bring it to a personal level. Describe what a job means to a family. As indicated in Chapter 1, during public comment sessions regarding policy decisions that would impact the continued operation of a manufacturing facility, I would often hear about the impact of a primary breadwinner of the family losing a job. What it means to have the breadwinner come home and say to the family: *I lost my job today.* The dread, the sense of foreboding, that accompanies that simple statement. The story can be told to employees through the voice of the spouse, or even more powerfully, through the voice of the children.

We need to make the connection for how something as simple as the creation of a job turns into something that changes many lives for the better. For example, how having a job translates into the hopes and dreams of an entire family. What does it mean in terms of going to college, the new computer, wedding plans, etc.?

Then look at it from the larger socio-economic perspective. What are the implications when a primary breadwinner loses a job in terms of likelihood of domestic or substance abuse, the consequences for their potential future earnings, and the highest education level their children will achieve? Don't take my word for this. Go to public meetings. Hear the stories for yourself. I heard them, and it changed the way I went about my job. I realized that every day in my work I was carrying around in my hands the hopes and dreams of ordinary citizens.

It is a powerful motivator when you have internalized the stories of how our work affects real people and can relate it in your own words, based on what you have heard directly from the public. You can explain the impact on people's lives as a result of accomplishing environmental mitigation. How it resulted in better health for nearby residents, their sense of empowerment as their living environment has been improved, the enhanced environmental safety for children who live nearby. The increase in nearby property values.

It is our job as public sector leaders to unleash the latent power of employee pride in public service. A leader must continually reinforce the merit in the mission. To make clear that every employee contributes to the large social goals that are the agency's mission, whether they are directly engaged in the field or providing accounting assistance or janitorial services. The mission cannot be accomplished without all the cogs of the wheel working together. Creating focus on meaningful outcomes leads to unleashing the power of public service. The ability to change people's lives for the better is a powerful tonic for an enervating world. Connection to purpose generates pride, which leads to a desire for better performance. that initiates the opposite of a viscous cycle—a *virtuous* cycle toward improved individual and agency performance.

At BPA employee meetings, I tried to be sure to talk about the ways our actions at work affected the quality of life for eleven million people in the Pacific Northwest. And then to bring it home in some way I had actually witnessed, where our people through initiative had made the world a better place for an individual, a family, or a community. Working at the local level, in Chelan, created many opportunities to display how our low electric rates, parks, and broadband access programs contributed to the well-being of community members.

Think about what you would want your employees to say if asked what they do. Do you want them to say I make sure the numbers add up or I track the number of widgets produced? Or would you want them to say I work at a place that contributes to improving the quality of life for you and all your friends, neighbors, and relatives? The power of the latter statement is the power of having employees who really care, who are performing quality work because they know it makes a difference. It is the power of pride.

This opportunity to provide public service is also in fact our best recruiting and retention strategy. Described correctly, it provides a psychic reward that can expand upon income. That power can also lower your attrition rate, helping to keep costs lower due to not having to train new people. It can help attract great talent when the monetary compensation options are inadequate.

Using connections to improve service

Creating connections to meaningful outcomes leads to a culture of continuously seeking to improve the services provided. Focusing on the importance of the outcome creates the motivation for working to make things better.

I once heard a story about a superintendent of a public school system that has stuck with me throughout my career. The district had a substantial quality-control problem with their printing. They tried offering their printer carrots and sticks, but teachers kept complaining the products they received were sub-standard. Then they tried one thing that made more difference than all their other efforts, combined. They had the printers deliver the products to the teachers, directly. The teachers receiving the material would review and critique with the printer standing there. Errors would be pointed out. *Look: I can't use this because a page is missing and the reading will make no sense*, or, *this page is out of order on the test.*

To the printers, the work became more than a job based on getting so many pages out by the end of the day. They saw that they were an important part of the learning process, a process that was severely disrupted when the quality of their work did not meet standards. The message here is to connect your employees to the importance of their work by physically connecting them to the end users. Or if that is not possible, provide your employees with visual examples of your customers' lives and how their lives are enhanced by the work the agency is engaged in. That very connection shows that their best, high-performance work is needed to succeed, by making real change.

Speaking out sincerely

I have found sincerity is not the biggest challenge for leaders. They believe in the mission. They believe in the importance of public service. The hardest thing for most leaders…is to talk about it. Particularly in today's culture that can be so dismissive of public service and servants, wearing your heart on your sleeve about the value created by public service can feel out of step. It's easier and more comfortable to go with resigned silence. Unfortunately, this makes the problem worse.

In my career, I often worried about being laughed at or dismissed when I began talking publicly about what I believed: That public service is a noble mission. That we can perform our jobs at levels that meet or exceed the standards of the private sector. And in fact, I did get some feedback that my message seemed naïve, particularly early in my leadership tenure. But I persevered, because it was sincere. It was what I believed in.

I also heard that there were many people whom it touched, and this feedback helped keep me going. My beliefs, when articulated, spoke to them about why they had chosen a career in public service. They could tell I was from the heart, that I believed what I was saying. They also understood that I was talking about how we had to change and continuously improve if we were going to live up to that high standard.

When I left BPA, I asked people for letters of remembrances they had of the time I had spent leading. By far, the most prevalent comment was how my commitment to public service motivated and inspired people in their day-to-day jobs. How it helped define the path when difficult choices needed to be made. How it gave them pride in their own work and the work of the agency. I could not have received a better gift.

Controversy as a positive

Public controversy can often be discouraging to employees because it is viewed as criticism of the agency's direction, an expression on the part of some people that the agency is not serving the public interest. This can be demoralizing. But unless agency personnel have engaged in unscrupulous or incompetent activity, it need not be.

Controversy regarding policy objectives should be embraced as evidence that your agency's work matters to the public. Being engaged in high-visibility disputes reflects how important our work is to the public. Disputes are often attempts by advocates to encourage the public to redefine the public interest. I told employees I would much rather work for an agency that matters to the public than one that does not. Controversy around your agency is an opportunity to create a greater sense for employees of the import of the work, and hence, the need to perform at high levels.

Encouraging subject matter mastery

We have another opportunity to create pride in the public sector that is often overlooked. We have technical experts on subjects that matter to the public. We produce analysis on subjects that go to the heart of impacts on communities that will affect people's everyday lives.

We should want our employees to be the best in their fields. People are motivated by the chance to become subject matter experts. When we combine training opportunities with motivation, we get highly skilled advisors to the public. These advisors can help citizens understand the impacts of various public policy choices on their lives. It's a virtuous cycle. Higher motivation leads to greater interest in training, and that leads to more effective employees who make better connections with the public. Ultimately, that generates more public support.

Conclusion

You may have seen linemen in action on cold winter days and wondered what kind of person has the moxie to do what they do. As a leader of electric utilities, it is inspiring to see the commitment to public service these folks have. When you ask linemen about their jobs, they are invariably humble, focusing on the knowledge that people are counting on them for comfort, and in some extreme cases, survival. They take pride in the importance of their work and their skill in accomplishing it.

Tapping into the power of pride through the motivation of public service is how we can best serve the public interest. Ultimately, our goal is to create pride. Pride, though, can only be deep seated if an agency successfully accomplishes its mission.

Part 2 turns to the management tools you can use to spread the influence of a focus on serving the public interest throughout an organization. This provides a systemic approach to integration of a public service culture within your organization.

Creating Structure with Public Service at the Core

3

Mission, Vision, and Values

You are not here merely to make a living. You are here in order for the world to live more amply, with greater vision, with a finer spirit of hope and achievement. You are here to enrich the world, and you impoverish yourself if you forget the errand.

—Woodrow Wilson

Early in my career, I was involved in a junior role supporting decisions on whether to terminate construction on partially built nuclear plants. These were difficult decisions with many components, not the least of which was that billions of dollars had already been spent on these plants. We were fortunate to have an inspiring leader who initiated a critical strategic retreat that included defining our mission and vision. At the time, however, I was aghast that we would "waste" time when the decisions that were pending had such critical relevance to the public.

I must admit that I spent years being among the many who believed that the definition of mission, vision, and values was highfalutin gobbledygook we did on management retreats—before we went back to the real work of defining policy and managing programs.

It was interesting intellectually in the midst of the process, but it seemed to lack a clear relevance to me. In fact, there were times when I actively resisted spending time on something so amorphous as agency values.

Over time, though, I came to realize that the time invested in defining these three culture-defining areas provided context and foundation for our work, extending the reach of the management team throughout the organization. It accelerated work because it provided staff direction beyond just...*bring me a rock.*

Mission, vision, and values can be used to create a focus on serving the public interest. There are many issues that must be dealt with in managing the agency on a day-to-day basis. But what I found is that over time many of those issues would be forgotten. What resonated across the agency was the strategic direction represented by mission, vision, and values. If done well, these were the things that employees remembered, connected to, and ultimately established the culture for the organization. Mission, vision, and values that explicitly incorporate public service values establish a cultural foundation for the organization.

Going back to the nuclear plant construction deliberation, our leader focused us on defining a vision statement that ended up being simple: *Best for the Northwest*. It was surprising how that reduced a lot of the discussion, honing the focus on political considerations about how our decisions would look. It redirected the discussion to what at that moment in time would be best for Pacific Northwest citizens—as defined by them.

KEY TAKEAWAYS

Mission, vision, and values create means to build a culture based on public service, establish priorities, and define how work gets done in the right way. Done right, mission, vision and values will be deeply motivational. They extend the reach of management's philosophy throughout the organization.

In the public sector, mission describes the most important functions to the public carried out by the organization. A great mission statement includes the fundamental public service purpose behind the organization's existence (the *why*), as well as its functions.

Vision provides the tool for defining in concise terms the high-level *outcomes* your organization is striving to achieve that serve the public interest.

Articulating values provides the opportunity to define *how* your mission and vision should be accomplished in a manner that consistently embraces serving the public interest.

Three values may be generally applicable across many governmental organizations: trustworthiness, stewardship, and operational excellence.

Establishing core values should be limited to a small memorable number so they will be widely used.

Establishing mission, vision, and values only sets the stage. The effectiveness is determined by whether organizational leaders explicitly reference their use in decision-making, especially when difficult issues are in play.

Mission: What and Why

Mission statements always focus on the most important roles the agency plays. Describing agency functions can seem like a waste of time to some, because, as the saying goes, *who around here doesn't know what it is that we do?* But creating or reshaping a mission statement engages a discussion of what is most important, and hence, helps to set priorities.

Once having defined a mission, choosing to change it takes on increasing importance. This is another advantage I did not recognize for quite some time in my career. This is particularly true if the mission statement is altered to add or subtract a function.

For example, at BPA we had a mission statement that was descriptive of the primary functions the agency was statutorily authorized to accomplish. Selling power and transmission services on a not for profit basis were the two fundamental missions of the agency, and thus, were stated clearly.

Revising the mission statement allowed us to make an important symbolic change that represented a fundamental shift in our agency priorities. Over a long period of time, the agency's responsibilities for mitigating for damage to fish and wildlife caused by the hydroelectric projects not only took on increasing importance and effort, it also engaged a substantially increasing share of the agency budget.

Accomplishing the agency's mitigation responsibility became a critical component of achieving success for all of our stakeholders: those who cared deeply about fish and wildlife, and those who cared deeply about our rate levels. Finally, it reached a point, based on what we were hearing from key stakeholders, where the importance of accomplishing the fish and wildlife mission rivaled that of the power and transmission mission.

In order to reflect the broad public interest, we chose to modify our mission statement to add the function of fish and wildlife restoration. Employees told me it was a powerful internal signal that our job, in terms of serving the public interest, had shifted. It made the employees in fish and wildlife feel more like an integral part of the organization, rather than an appendage. It also signaled to other parts of the organization how important the fish and wildlife responsibilities had become.

Moving mission from good to great

Moving a mission statement from good to great means going beyond describing what an agency *does*. Articulating the "why" we exist right is where emotions and motivation become engaged. At Chelan, our board went beyond the important roles the agency plays using strategy and logic; it also emphasized engagement of the "heart." to explain *why* the agency exists. It brought to the forefront the public service focus that is the fundamental mission of the agency.

Chelan's mission statement begins with, *To enhance the quality of life in Chelan County*, and then speaks to the roles the agency plays. That simple precursor became a powerful measure of the quality of every decision, as well as priority setting. Did it meet the test of enhancing the quality of life for the people we served?

Vision

Defining a vision creates another opportunity to reinforce the theme of the primacy of public service. More so than a mission statement, the vision is usually a short, pithy expression of what outcomes are really important to the organization.

Vision statements are worth arguing over. A vision statement needs to engage the most fundamental arguments in the agency about what drives decisions. Once adopted, they should last, and not only help define, but also energize your corporate culture.

The vision statement was a struggle for many years at BPA. Are we a business or are we a public sector agency? As a business, we might worry less about equitable treatment of stakeholders, and our budget decisions might focus less on distributional benefits. We might focus more on maximizing our potential financial gains in markets. This was a constant source of friction in the agency: *who are we really?*

Ultimately, we chose to embrace both concepts, but to place a higher emphasis on our public sector responsibilities. There are many utilities across the country that operate as private sector businesses. Our belief was that what made us unique and worthy of being created and maintained in federal statute were the public responsibilities entrusted to us.

The vision we chose? *Accomplishing our public responsibilities through a commercially successful business.* We put public responsibilities first to reflect public service as our highest priority and what separated us from the private sector. Then we defined our public responsibilities as: keeping rates low, maintaining high electric-system reliability, being responsible environmental stewards, and being accountable to the people we served.

Yet the statement also recognized that BPA's only source of operating funds is through selling power and transmission services. If BPA is going to retain the honor of meeting the public's needs, it has to be a successful participant in the electric power and transmission marketplace.

A vision statement should describe your predilection for where priorities should be placed. But even when you gain this greater clarity about fundamental purposes for the agency, your vision statement should not resolve all issues for all time. If your vision statement is written to end all debate, it will risk the failure of there being only one way to solve for serving the public interest; experience shows that the approach is always multi-faceted.

Our debates at BPA over the new vision statement at BPA substantially reduced what had seemed like an interminable debate about whether we should be tilted toward one end of the spectrum or the other. It also provided guidance for policy discussions in the agency, by leaning more heavily on our public responsibilities as our guiding light.

At Chelan, we confronted a different issue. There was clarity around our public service mission being the highest priority. But there had been debates about short-term vs long-term priorities. Yet, the history of the biggest successes in the organization had been when the focus was on creating long-term value over short-term needs. That led to the adoption of a simple vision statement, to create the "best value for the most people for the longest period of time." That simple statement became the standard for all decisions brought forward to the board, particularly when they were difficult or controversial.

Values

I have found that many of my initial instincts about establishing management structures were imperfect. Probably the area that I most resisted, but ultimately found great benefit in, was in establishing agency values. I did not understand how establishing values was going to help us get our work done. It seemed like an overhead time-sink. A fellow employee captured my feelings: "Do you think we are valueless?" she asked. "What void are you trying to fill?"

The answer was no, we are not valueless. But if we are not clear about what is most important, then we are rudderless when it comes to *how* we make decisions. Establishing values helped assure that we would go about solving problems within an aligned framework.

Defining values will cause at least some in your organization to wonder whether management believes there is a significant problem that needs to be solved. Sometimes there may be. An agency that has had an ethics crisis, for example, may need to add a specific ethics value. Other times, value selection can be a way to strengthen and solidify what may already be an organizational necessity: performing in a manner that generates trust, for example.

Values should reflect the characteristics that reinforce the responsibilities of serving the public interest. What are the values most important that the people in your organization must display in order for the organization to be successful?

Three Examples of Values

If you want to tap into the power of pride in public service, one must start with what values are necessary to best serve the public interest.

Within the public sector there are three interconnected concepts that are likely applicable to every organization: trustworthiness, operational excellence, and stewardship.

Defining trust in the public sector

Trust is composed of competence, integrity, and collaborative relationships:

Competence, because I'm not going to trust someone to work on my car who is not qualified. The same philosophy should be true for someone responsible for operating government. The competence component of trust is interconnected with the need for operational excellence. By choosing trust as a value, we are implicitly committing to investments in people and systems that will produce an effective and efficient organization.

Integrity, because trust is based on confidence that actions taken by government officials are based on serving the public interest, not self-interest. Ethics is a cornerstone of integrity (see more in Chapter 9 about ethics). Integrity also includes building confidence in the organizational commitment to sincerity and honesty—elements that are necessary for trusting relationships.

Collaborative relationships, because we as humans show more patience and give more grace to people who we know well enough to believe we understand their motivations, as long as they are sincere and honest.

The path to long-lasting success in the public sector is dependent on building trust. Competence is the necessary foundation. Integrity is the bridge between competence and collaborative relationships. Collaborative relationships are the vehicles for building policies that enjoy broad support, and are durable for the long-term.

Being trustworthy requires operational excellence

To be trustworthy an organization needs to be competent. To be competent an organization needs to pursue operational excellence.

In the definition used here, operational excellence is about the day-to-day running of government, the fundamentals of what we do. It is the delivery of products and services that the public experiences either directly, or hears about indirectly in terms of efficiency and effectiveness. It often only gets serious attention when something goes wrong.

While it is frustrating, we should acknowledge there is tremendous public distrust that government can operate efficiently and effectively. There is a media bias to accentuate things that go wrong in government, while underreporting on government work successfully accomplished. There is the challenge of working in large organizations that because of checks and balances designed into the system can move slowly. It can be difficult to get resources to adopt new service-enhancing technologies. Personnel systems can make it difficult to use carrots and sticks to incent performance.

Yet, we also have a workforce that is tired of being looked upon as unable to competently perform. We have employees who want to be subject-matter experts. We have a public that is hungering for us to find new ways to do business that improves service and reduces costs.

We can choose to focus on our disadvantages, or we can choose to use our advantages to proactively seek to change the opinion of what government can accomplish within our sphere of influence.

The key is creating and supporting a culture focused on high quality of service to the public. To establish an expectation that a part of everyone's job is delivering high-quality products and services. A culture that celebrates service quality success, and focuses attention on disappointments, to achieve continuous improvement.

Signaling operational excellence is a high priority by making it a core value takes advantage of opportunity arising from instilling pride built upon serving the public interest. Increased employee pride leads to increased personal ownership to improve service, which can be fueled with management commitment to supporting operational excellence.

Pursuing operational excellence is enhanced when employees can see the meaningfulness of their work's impact on the public. It is a leader's job to either explain—or even better, show—employees how their jobs connect to serving the public (recall the example of the Minneapolis Public Schools).

In addition, adopting operational excellence as a core value helps commit an organization to providing employees the resources that lead to increased efficiency and effectiveness. For example, the opportunity to develop mastery of subject matter is highly motivational. When provided excellent training, technology, and tools, we unlock employee potential to provide excellent service to the public.

Continuous improvement to achieve operational excellence

We have reactive and proactive tools to support continuous improvement. In chapter 8, there is a discussion of the use of *root cause analysis* and *lessons learned exercises* that describes some of the reactive tools that can be used to improve performance. Better yet, though, are proactive tools, such as benchmarking

Benchmarking performance against other entities that perform similar work provides an objective test on how well basic functions are accomplished.

The use of benchmarking in the public sector should be thoughtfully expanded, even if just across government agencies. Concerns will invariably arise about the comparability of functions across agencies, discouraging the use of benchmarking right from the start. I tended to worry less about whether the functions were exactly comparable, since comparison data of efficiency or effectiveness are not what is most valuable. Where true value lies in benchmarking are the very questions that people begin to ask about why our products or services are doing better or worse than others. The blinders come off when employees look

"While it may not be obvious early in your career, the farther up the management chain you proceed, the greater the value of establishing mission, vision, and values."

outside their own organization. People get thinking about opportunities to create a better world. Even an imperfect benchmarking exercise will still generate this benefit.

Benchmarking benefits from us generally acting as competitive beings—and that includes all employees, from leadership to entry-level administration Comparing our operation against others gets an organization out of the mindset that "we are great at what we do" that is easy to fall into—if there are no comparisons against similarly situated organizations.

Often, however, it is hard to get started on benchmarking for your entire organization, due to budget considerations, or internal resistance. A step in the right direction is strongly encouraging managers to find people with similar duties completely outside their organization (in the private or public sector), in order to form peer-sharing relationships. It's helpful just to have someone to talk to who shares common challenges. It opens the door to considering new approaches that might otherwise have been too far outside of the box.

Utilizing technology to support operational excellence

If we are to enhance the public's view of its government, we are going to need to go beyond just the consideration of policy. We must improve the quality of product delivery and service that the public experiences. That will take unleashing the creativity of our entire workforce and increasing attention on managing to results based on what the public wants from their government.

As the technology revolution expands around us, a commitment to improving the quality of the customer's experience is particularly important. We can see the pace of change in technology is accelerating in our daily lives. For example, people want to communicate on mobile devices at their convenience. Government is going to need to keep up, or lose trust. That requires the hard work of advocating for budget and staff for systems improvements, which are not as alluring as policy initiatives.

A commitment to operational excellence is a commitment to embracing change. But change, particularly change in the use of technology, which fundamentally gets to business systems and processes, is difficult for the people in any organization. Change management processes need to be established to be successful. Change management sounds hard, but really has a simple core: Communicate frequently *why* change is being implemented, focused on the value to the public. Be open to bidirectional communication about the *how* the change will be implemented, as long as the goal of improving service to the public is the primary objective.

Choosing to establish a core value around the concept of operational excellence makes the core work a greater priority. It tells your organization that the day-to-day delivery of service to the public is important, and that it will get attention proactively—not just after something goes wrong.

Integrity is the bridge to collaborative relationships

Being competent is the foundation to building collaborative relationships. Acting with integrity is the structure of the house. First and foremost to integrity is assuming the role of public service. Putting aside self-interest to focus on what best serves the public. This is not easy in a society that encourages individual entrepreneurialism. In fact, the benefit of the doubt in our society is that government officials are focused on themselves first. We have to prove otherwise through our actions. Only through persistent, continuous, sincere commitment to actions and decisions reflecting the public interest are we able to build respect for our integrity.

Building a reputation for integrity, whether at the individual or organizational level, also requires a commitment to honesty. Honesty, though, can be difficult to accomplish in all circumstances. Often people will take you into their confidence providing information that is valuable but not intended to be shared. Honesty does not mean always telling everything you know. It does mean not saying something that is wrong. It sometimes requires saying, I can't say more about that without violating a confidence.

Trustworthiness is built on collaborative relationships

Building collaborative relationships that are founded on trust takes time and effort. Assume it is part of the job to get out regularly and talk to stakeholders, even if there is not a specific subject in mind. It is particularly important to open the door to those who have a different point of view, to find where there may be common ground. Without solid efforts to engage stakeholders, even the best possible outcomes will not get an A for performance from them.

For example, we had regularly scheduled informal sessions at BPA with key stakeholders in which they knew anyone could bring up whatever issues might be on their mind. They were invited even if they were litigating against us, although we tried to minimize the engagement of attorneys. These personal connections are as important as the substantive discussions because of who we are as humans. We are more interested and willing to solve problems with people we enjoy being around, rather than those we do not know. Building these relationships outside of a crisis moment makes them more useful when they are needed.

Building collaboration starts with listening

Building collaborative relationships takes a willingness to really listen. Really listening means focusing entirely on what the person is saying, and not thinking about what you are going to say next. It's about understanding, not winning the argument.

Beginning counselors are taught the skill of reflecting back what they have heard as the first response to an important statement. It's a useful skill for public servants. This helps make sure you have understood the comment, gives the other person the chance to correct or add clarification to their statement, and gives you time to respond with greater use of your intellect than your emotion.

I wanted our people to be thinking as much about whether they were building long-term collaborative relationships, both internally and externally, in their day-to-day interactions as they were thinking about accomplishing that day's assignment. This reflected the belief that if we were good as an organization at building collaborative relationships, it would enhance our ability to accomplish our mission more quickly. As Steven M. Covey, author of *The Speed of Trust*, puts it, "things go faster when there is trust than when there is not." Collaboration creates common ground that can avoid or even settle litigation.

Moreover, our interactions with stakeholders move from issue to issue. If we get past one issue in a way that leaves a stakeholder feeling battered, it is almost certain there will be another one that will come up where there will be the opportunity for retribution. This is particularly true when someone believes they have not been respected. The absolute key to building collaborative relationships is using the golden rule of treating people with the same respectful treatment we would want for ourselves.

Stewardship defined

Stewardship goes a step beyond being trustworthy by focusing on the motivation for action.

Acting as stewards gets us out of the mode of thinking about the decision as *what do I think is the best outcome?* and more into *what does the public believe is the best course?*.

Embracing a stewardship philosophy can be a radical change for an organization. There are many technical experts throughout government who believe they can best define the path based on their expertise. When I first entered government in 1981, this was the prevalent view, based on how things had worked in the past. *The public is paying us to be the technical experts, defining issues, and providing the answers*, sums it up.

But there has been an evolution that has radically changed what people want from their government. People today have substantially higher levels of education than in the past. As a result, the public's ability to comprehend complex subject matter is greater than in the past. They are less willing to just defer to designated technical government expertise.

In addition, the information explosion has put reams of information at people's fingertips. In fact, there is so much out there that it has become nearly impossible for any one individual, including a government employee whose full-time job it may be to compile the information, to see and comprehend everything relevant to the decision.

As a result, government employees must think differently about the extent to which we facilitate conversation, versus provide technical expertise. It is no longer our role to merely present complex material and a conclusion based on our expertise. Rather, we must present the technical information we have and then seek to supplement it with information the public can provide, working collaboratively toward the best interests of the public.

A steward understands their job is to best reflect the will of the people who have turned over control of their assets. This requires soliciting and being deferential to the views of those who have given us their trust. On the large public scale, this can be difficult to comprehend because of the cacophony of voices. The challenge is to separate your subjective beliefs from the collective will of the people.

When stewardship seems to conflict with public will

Being a steward is not easy. There will be many times when the will of the people seems to either ignore a long-term public interest perspective, or minority opinions are being shouted down. These two types of issues deserve different types of responses:

In the first case, it becomes our responsibility as government officials to make sure the information about long-term consequences is broadly available. If the public understands this, and still wants a short-term focus, it is our duty to reflect the will of the people. That is what democracy is about. We either trust in our democratic form of government—based on the will of the public—or we do not. If we cannot countenance the public will, then it may be time to leave government service.

As to the latter problem, frequently the law will protect minority rights. If that is not enough, however, the challenge is to protect minority opinions as best we can through education. Being trustworthy stewards means working for all the public. Our challenge in this situation is to seek to understand the perspective of the minority and try to identify means to address their concerns, without losing the support of the majority.

We can attempt to do that through bilateral discussions with both sides, or bring the sides together to find common ground. We can share the perspective of the aggrieved minority party in an empathetic way, to assure the majority hears the concern. We can shine a public spotlight on the issue to test whether that might further engage the public, or even change the minds of some.

Even if common ground seems unachievable, at a minimum we should strive to achieve the sense that everyone was heard, and that we sought every possible avenue to find common ground that would allow all parties to live with the conclusion.

Limiting the number of values

Choosing values can easily lead to so many values being adopted as to make the exercise meaningless. If employees cannot remember the values, they are supposed to use to guide how decisions will be made, then they are likely not being used to create alignment.

It's hard to be against a long list of valuable values (who can be against respect, integrity etc.?). But any exercise to establish values should start with a commitment to a maximum number that is adhered to and can be remembered. That's why the term *core* values is used to differentiate from all the values that may be relevant.

When I arrived at Chelan there were seven adopted values. I informally surveyed twenty employees, including senior leaders, and nobody could name the values without resorting to reference documents. It seemed to me the values were not driving how the work got done. The senior team cut the number to four and defined metrics for increasing our employees' ability to remember the values. Within three years, we were able to eliminate the metrics, as the vast majority of employees could recite them.

Making our values meaningful

Critical to making values effective is how leaders talk about the decisions we are charged with making. Especially internally. If we, even in an off-handed way, make fun of public input, we send the wrong signal and undermine the culture we are seeking to create. Humor is useful in the workplace, but not when it undercuts our objectives. In all our communications, it is important to consistently show that we honor the input of the public.

How we resolve internal conflicting objectives provides definition to our commitment to values. For example, let's consider the use of delegated authority. There can be a positive tendency for managers to want to support our people who work for us, and their decisions. Yet, our employees can sometimes submit work that does not reflect adequate consideration of the public's views. At that moment it's important to be clear about your own values, with respect to what the responsibilities of government service encompasses. Sure, we might be confronted with the argument that a good manager supports their troops. But, the most important objective is serving the public, and that sometimes means sending the team back to develop a solution that is consistent with being a trustworthy steward.

It should also be a personal lesson: the team's assignment should have been more clearly established at the beginning, highlighting the value of being a trustworthy steward.

Making it real

A great deal of work can be invested to define mission, vision, and values. The outcomes of these efforts invariably end up on posters on the walls of meeting rooms and the like. But the value of these efforts is reaped only if key agency leaders point to how the mission, vision, and/or values were used to help guide their decisions.

For example, we had a strong set of commissioners at Chelan. When difficult decisions were pending, they would point to the wall and reflect on how they interpreted the mission or vision statement, with regard to the question at hand. It became clear to all employees that recommendations needed to be made in the context of what actions were most consistent with the mission and vision. The resulting alignment led to nearly all votes the commission took being unanimous.

Conclusion

While it may not be obvious early in your career, the farther up the management chain you proceed, the greater the value of establishing mission, vision, and values. Doing so extends the reach of executive management throughout the organization. An organizational culture that treasures its public service mission, using it to improve motivation and organizational performance, starts with incorporating public service values into its mission, vision and values. Then leadership explicitly uses them to make decisions. The results increase the odds of durable solutions to difficult public policy challenges.

4

Turning Mission, Vision, and Values into Strategy

The task of the leader is to get the people from where they are to where they have not been.

—Henry Kissinger

Early in my career, I had the opportunity to represent my agency in Washington, DC. I was able to create a strong working relationship with a member of Congress and his staff. That led to introducing a piece of legislation that was beneficial to the agency and many of its customers. I can be competitive, and I really wanted to make this legislation happen. So much so that I could not see the amount of resistance that was forming. When the legislation came to the House floor as an amendment, it was rejected—with the opposition led by a representative important to our overall agency strategy. The issue became characterized as partisan, which was fundamentally at odds with our agency mission to operate in a way that served *all* the people of the Northwest.

Fortunately, the damage to the relationship with the opposing side was temporary. That said, in my zeal to make a positive difference with what I believed was a good idea, I had done damage to our overall agency success by losing sight of our mission and how our strategy fit within that mission.

Strategy is ultimately about resource allocation: dollars and people. Strategy defined by the organization's mission, vision, and values helps focus the allocation of resources on the ideas that will create the greatest value for the organization and the people it serves. There are many, many ideas out there that look good on a stand-alone basis, but can do damage to the larger strategy of the organization. Widely

39

communicated and understood strategy helps leaders and staff pinpoint and deliver on the most important initiatives. For example, a not-for-profit organization that is initiating a capital campaign may not want to take on an important, but controversial, issue that drives some members away if the capital campaign is the highest strategic priority.

As a leader it is your responsibility to guide the development, communication, and implementation of the strategy. This is true no matter what level you operate at in the organization. Your leaders may define strategic sideboards for where they want to go that become the foundation for your actions. Yet, there are degrees of freedom for both what should be accomplished, and how. That is your responsibility to define.

KEY TAKEAWAYS

A key difference in public versus private-sector strategic planning is the focus on serving the public interest, including creating space to allow the public to participate in setting the course.

There are five stages in effective public sector strategic planning: setting the context; public engagement; translating public input into a plan with strategic objectives; implementing the plan through defining a Balanced Scorecard restructured for the public sector; and, establishing metrics-driven performance plans.

Begin the strategic planning process by setting the context for the public as to what's relevant and possible. Engage the public in ways that will allow them to provide useful input and guidance about what's important to their lives. Turn the input into a plan that includes a small number of key strategic objectives. Engage employees utilizing their specific expertise.

Use a Balanced Scorecard approach to assure your plan addresses the elements necessary for successful implementation. Your group, whatever size, will benefit from having a comprehensive strategy that addresses the perspectives of stakeholders, financial, internal processes, and people/culture.

Strategy for a public sector organization starts with putting the stakeholder perspective as the primary driver of agency success. The other perspectives are aligned to drive success in stakeholder satisfaction. Excellent means for measuring stakeholder satisfaction are necessary.

The financial perspective must at a minimum assure managing to budget is accomplished, for legal reasons, and to avoid triggering the cultural perspective prevalent in our society that government cannot manage to budget.

We need to not let the public's focus on evolving policy issues overwhelm the need to actively manage day-to-day operational issues like filling the potholes in the streets. Operations failures take more time to repair and do more damage than policy failures. Seek out the processes for improvement that have the greatest impact on the public. Use technology to improve processes, but with more planning and budget control than in the private sector.

The people and culture element is unique in the public sector. Options for action include reinforcing agency core values through personnel selection processes, supporting subject-matter mastery, celebrating great individual public service, addressing poor performance, and better connecting employees to the people they serve.

Public Sector Strategy

Early in my tenure as the BPA CEO, I would get the question: What is your strategy? In those days, I was fortunate that I had the word "acting" in front of my title, because it allowed me to say that I was just trying to get us through the travails associated with what had become the west coast energy crisis. During that time, I realized how much people up and down the chain of command were looking for a comprehensive and logical set of interconnected actions that provided a sense of direction.

Strategy is a step more refined than mission and vision, focusing on a two to five-year time frame, but a step up from the specific metrics that are used to measure annual performance. A good strategy seeks to recognize the patterns where difficult issues intersect to find higher-level solutions. When defining strategy in the public sector, the foundation should be rooted in defining and achieving the public's interests. There are structured means to accomplish this.

Developing a public sector strategic plan

All strong organizations, whether in the public or private sector, are managed through a strategic plan. Clear definitions of outcomes align organizational efforts, thus creating the best opportunities for success.

There are many similarities between public and private sector strategic plans, but an important way that they are different is that in the public sector a strategic plan is based on what best serves the public interest. There is no effective way to address this without engaging the public to test concepts and, ultimately, seek public support. Effective public engagement on a strategic plan requires more than just calling a public meeting, however.

There are five stages in effective public sector strategic planning: set the context; public engagement; translating public input into a plan with strategic objectives; implementing the plan through defining a Balanced Scorecard restructured for the public sector; and establishing metrics-driven performance plans. The public is actively involved in the first three. The latter two are managed internally, while ensuring public transparency.

Set the context

It is the agency's responsibility to set the appropriate context. Without a concerted effort, the public does not have ready access to the foundational information regarding what is possible to include in a strategic plan. Nor does the public necessarily see the array of issues confronting a public sector organization, since their focus is likely only on the issues the agency is addressing that directly affects them.

A strong strategic planning exercise begins with providing the public the background information that allows them to engage in a meaningful way. Many public comment sessions on public sector strategic plans have foundered due to a lack of established context. Staff rejects comments from the public as not founded in reality, but that's because the reality was not established at the beginning. If the public is asked how to create a better world, they will have lots of ideas. But those ideas need to be centered on the actions within the authorities and capabilities of the agency.

To have effective conversations with the public, there should be a kick-off to public engagement that establishes situational awareness. Setting goals for a strategic plan requires a basic understanding of the status and what is within the realm of the possible. The status defines the state of the most critical issues the organization is tasked with addressing. For an organization charged with delivering electric power, this was relatively easy to identify. The public cares about rates, reliability, environmental protection, and customer satisfaction. There are generally established metrics and frequently benchmark data that can be used to describe the status. From that basis, thoughts can be generated about opportunities for improvement.

The definition of opportunities available to public sector organizations are formed, at least partially, by statutory, financial, political, or workforce limitations. These limitations are not meant to be immutable, but instead represent what can be expected without extraordinary action, such as new legislation. For example, the current and forecasted financial position of the agency is necessary for effective public engagement. Constituents often have dreams about ways to create a better world that are not realistic, considering the financial resources available to the agency. Laying out the currently available financial resources and what can be reasonably forecasted helps to establish meaningful sideboards. Similarly, the agency's statutory authority establishes current boundaries on the types of activities that can be considered. Generating new financial resources or statutes is always possible, but the degree of difficulty should be acknowledged.

A financial or statutory conversation can easily lead to a testing of the sideboards as to whether, with additional political support, a limitation can be expanded through legislative action. A situational assessment of the constraints for an authorizing body (e.g., Constitutional limits, overall fiscal concerns, other priorities) helps put the public more in the shoes of decision-makers. It provides information about the level of difficulty associated with various options that may be proposed. These do not have to be detailed treatises, but general outlines of the current state.

There public should also be made aware of the current capabilities of the organization. All organizations have core competencies and strengths in operations and/or technology. Often, strategic plans lead to desires for stretching an organization to new areas. It's important for there to be a tactful presentation of the state of skills and capability to adopt new technologies reflecting reality—without demotivating staff.

Finally, there should be a description of the major challenges the organization faces. Sometimes, this can allow a discussion of where there

"Government cannot be run like a business because the objectives are fundamentally different."

are patterns within the challenges. These can be the most rewarding conversations; they often create opportunities for resolving multiple issues which, if addressed individually, are more difficult and time-consuming to solve. Picking where to provide emphasis is a judgment of agency leaders focused on what areas the public is most likely wanting to explore.

Context setting is a critical stage of strategic planning in the public sector. A skillful leader will anticipate the issues likely to come up in public comment on a strategic plan. Context setting is not a matter of describing every fact about the organization. It is focused on the issues that are most likely to be in play during the planning process. Context setting does not decide for the public what's important, but does try to anticipate key issues to seed the conversation.

Setting context is best accomplished through a written document and/or video that the public can review at their convenience. It's also valuable to have a kick-off meeting with interested stakeholders so they all hear it at the same time and can share thoughts and questions.

Public Engagement

Having set the context, it's now time for the public to have their chance. This can be accomplished, in part, through large public meetings. From my perspective, however, these are a necessary, but far from sufficient means, to engage the public. They *check the box* that public comment has been gathered, but frequently don't lead to better understanding of the public's interest, when the agency's capabilities are considered. It's also often difficult to improve the public's understanding of the complexities of the agency's decisions. The larger the meeting, the harder it is to allow a conversation to evolve into deeper understanding that occurs through dialogue. Members of the public make their statements in random ways, based on lining up at a microphone, making it difficult to pursue the meaning of their comments and share relevant information.

To better engage the public, consider finding means to define specific interests that commenters have, then based on those shared interests, break the larger crowd into smaller groups that operate simultaneously, in lieu of the large meeting. Also, small groups willing to put in significant time for engaged dialogue can be very effective. If context setting has been prescient, the issues for the groups to wrestle with can be defined early in the process. But the unexpected happens, and then a new work group focus may be added, or alternatively, a refocusing of the existing work groups. What's critical is that the groups are given options to wrestle with, not conclusions to test.

Merely making it clear that it will, for example, take a ten-hour commitment to participate in these small groups helps to separate those who want to be heard (which must be allowed) from those who want to dig in to find viable strategies. Now, this is a significant time commitment on the part of the agency, as well, but the result is working with a select group of the public who are truly interested in understanding and wanting viable strategies. This can also translate in the end into a group of advocates for the planning process, or even the agency and its mission. At Chelan, for instance, our most vocal proponents for our adopted strategic plan came out of these kind of work groups.

There is always the risk of the *loudmouth* who dominates discussion in small groups. This risk can be mitigated through good planning up front to establish group norms, enforced by the group, regarding process issues such as how speaking time is shared.

Establish means for everyone to participate

While we need in-depth participation by some, there also need to be avenues for those with limited time, but who still are interested enough in the issue at hand to offer their views. A broad but short priorities survey can provide a tool to make this happen. The challenge is to not ask people just what they want, but how to set priorities. Asking people what they want leads to a large agenda that lacks ability to resource it. A tool we used at Chelan is to survey for a variety of different priorities giving respondents ten *coins* they could use. Respondents could spend all their coins for one priority, or spread them around. Priorities ranged from *keep rates as low as possible* to *new amenities for the benefit of the community*. Although not a random sample, as it was provided to all our customer-owners, it provided valuable information about the priorities the community put on various public benefits we could provide.

Translating public input into a plan with strategic objectives

Now comes the most difficult part for the leader. There will be lots of input from the public, as well as from the people you report to. It's time to translate this input into focused outcomes. Three is best, five at most. The plan must be encompassing enough to address the array of the most pertinent public comments. It must also reflect the views represented by your elected leaders, who represent the public. It must be specific enough to allow budgets and programs to be developed that reflect the guidance in the plan.

Here's an example with three main objectives from Chelan when this approach became clearer to me:

- Reduce debt: This was a clear statement, if difficult to accomplish. The public and the elected board believed debt versus equity had grown too large.

- Invest in assets and people: As an infrastructure-based organization, creating *best for the most for the longest* required physical capital investments to refurbish and grow. It also required new technology adoption and skills by the workforce. This committed the organization to increased spending for these objectives.

- Invest in public benefits: The public wanted investments in activities that did not necessarily have a positive business case, but would enhance the quality of life. But this had to be managed against the risk of raising rates. The conclusion was to define a program for public benefit projects where all the ideas competed against each other for a limited amount of funds, with the funds available being determined by overall financial performance.

Having three strategic objectives greatly simplified communicating with the public. Every speech and all our primary communication vehicles referenced the three strategic objectives. It was comprehensible to the public. Yet at the same time, it was specific enough to create clear direction for the implementation plans that would follow.

The powerful value of the strategic plan resulted in the support from the public as the plan was implemented. The development and approval of our budget documents became easier as long as the substance matched the plan, and particularly, the strategic objectives. In a second version of the strategic plan, even raising rates became less controversial, as a dedicated conversation about rates was included in the public comment and work group processes.

Employee Engagement

While facing outward toward the public in the planning process is the priority, there is also a need to face inward. Employees should have the opportunity to influence the process. It's important, though, that employee voices do not dominate the view of the public due to their subject matter expertise.

It's also necessary to have the plan consider the administrative elements. Employees best understand what will be necessary for the plan to succeed. Things like priority setting, budget development, staffing, skill development, and process improvements. Fortunately, there is a tool that helps to organize thoughts about organizing to implement the plan. It's the *Balanced Scorecard*, as modified to reflect a focus on serving the public interest.

Using a Balanced Scorecard approach

The Balanced Scorecard (with the ignominious acronym BS that amuses every strategic planning session where it is employed) has become a ubiquitous tool for businesses to help establish their strategy. It simply is a systematic way to assure an across-the-board look at the elements of the successful strategy for any organization. If you are not already familiar with the BS approach, there are many good online resources readily available with a quick search. The BS is an important tool to assure your strategic plan will actually be implemented.

Review your plan against the four key elements identified in the BS to identify key, big-picture outcomes that are necessary for the strategy to succeed. While different names are used in various publications, my preferences follow: the financial, stakeholder, internal processes, and people/culture perspectives.

BS, however, was built around a private-sector model focused appropriately on profit and loss. With one important change, the value of BS can be brought to the public sector.

Switching the focus of the Balanced Scorecard

The four perspectives are frequently depicted in the form of swim lanes. The top swim lane is what is most important to business—the financial perspective, focused on profit and loss. That is undergirded by second, the stakeholder perspective that reflects customers and other stakeholders who impact the success of the business.

Third is the internal processes that define how the work gets done and, for many businesses, is the key to establishing and maintaining a market niche. How does the product get produced in a unique way that is hard for others to replicate?

Finally, there is the people and culture perspective. This defines what kind of values, along with skills and talent, that are necessary for the business to be successful.

Frequently, we hear in the public discourse that government should be run like a business. There are significant similarities in terms of the importance of defining strategy between government and the private sector. These similarities allow for management tools to be used inter-changeably, or with modest modifications, between the sectors. But government cannot be run like a business because the objectives are fundamentally different. The BS points out likely the most significant difference between government and business. Governmental organizations and NGOs do not exist primarily to create a profit for a select group. The financial perspective is not the most important.

Instead, the not-for-profits exist primarily to create a better life for the public than would occur in their absence. The best measure of success is stakeholder satisfaction. The word stakeholder is used to mean all members of the public impacted by the agency's decisions. The bottom line is whether the public believes it is receiving value from the organization.

Hence, the key change to be made is to switch the top two swim lanes: To place the stakeholder perspective on top as the ultimate goal to be achieved, while the financial swim lane moves down to the second position.

Sometimes, this switching of the two swim lanes, financial and stakeholder perspectives, is perceived as meaning that the financial component is not important. That would be an incorrect conclusion. It is no truer than if private sector businesses did not have to be concerned with what their customers and stakeholders think about them because all they care about is profit and loss. The financial and stakeholder perspectives are intermingled in both the private and public sectors. The difference is only, and importantly, a matter of emphasis.

Focusing on stakeholder satisfaction as the topmost goal creates clarity and consistency around the message that as a public sector organization, we are focused on serving the public interest as our primary goal. One of the key benefits of the BS is to create clarity about why organizationally we do the things we do. The structure is designed to create focus on actions that lead to accomplishing the goals in the topmost swim lane.

The importance of the top of the scorecard

I am loathe to admit this as a long-time career civil servant, but all too often we as government workers lose sight of why we are here. We lose sight of the fact that we exist only to serve the public. How many of us have experienced the lack of respectful treatment from a government worker when we have been seeking a service, frequently one required by the government? How many of us have experienced the frustration of being transferred around from public servant to public servant with no sense that anyone is taking accountability to get the problem solved? How often have we been confronted with a situation that it feels like we are not perceived as a customer?

If we want to work in a profession that is respected, or even revered, we must earn it. We have to understand that we are going to engage with a public that can be frustrated, yet not respond in kind with frustration. We must view ourselves and our people as problem solvers on behalf of the public. We have to actively seek out the views of the public we serve and improve their experience in dealing with us.

Beyond customer service, we also must understand how the public is defining its interest. Investors know that they need to be constantly watching financial markets because movements occur in unexpected ways. Similarly, those of us who are engaging in the public sector must be observant of shifts in public opinion. One should enjoy staying in touch with how the public interest is shifting, in order to serve it. Elections provide the most important measure of public attitude shifts, but there are other tools including conversations with elected officials (more on this in Chapters 10 and 11) and stakeholders, economic and environmental data, and emerging public focus on issues related to those your agency is engaged in.

Measuring stakeholder satisfaction

To create clarity around desired outcomes, one must have measurable goals with respect for the stakeholder perspective. This is a great challenge of working in the public sector. In the private sector, there are clear measures of success in terms of financial performance. Measuring stakeholder satisfaction as the most important outcome is much more difficult.

At BPA and Chelan, we used satisfaction surveys (different from the priority surveys mentioned earlier in this chapter) conducted either annually or biannually to help us understand our success in meeting the needs of the public. A survey instrument can provide lots of data about various elements of your program service. But there are two key things you must do. First, there must be an overall question that asks stakeholders to rate their level of satisfaction. Second, the survey must be short enough (no more than fifteen minutes, preferably less) that your key stakeholders will choose to participate year after year.

There are two kinds of satisfaction surveys: First, engaging the general public the agency impacts through a random sample. Second, a more focused survey of key stakeholders who are knowledgeable about the agency. For the latter, it is key to get a cross sample of influential people who will most influence the future direction of the agency. For example, key members of the executive and legislative branches who influence the program should be included. These could be staff members, or the actual elected official, if they are willing. These two categories are particularly important because they represent the publicly elected officials, and hence, are the representatives of the public. I would often place more weight on their responses because of their significance in establishing policy.

The feedback from these groups alone, though, will mostly represent a *lagging indicator*, for by the time executive or legislative branch leaders engage in a problem, there is likely a substantial stakeholder concern that has been growing for a while. Put another way, the dam has been leaking for some time and the repairs will be more difficult to put in place.

Program direction needs to be guided by *leading indicators*, as well. The best leading indicators are the stakeholders who are closest to the program. That includes both proponents and opponents of program activities. Elected officials are heavily dependent upon the input of these groups for information about the state of the program. Moreover, these are the people who are often most impacted by the program you are managing for the benefit of the public.

Defining whom to survey is your purview. Do not succumb to the desire to survey only the people you know are happy with the program. It may make you feel good, but the data are otherwise useless to you, not providing the leading indicator of problems that can help you avoid much more serious problems later. And it will not do much good to tell people that your satisfaction scores are high while constituents are meanwhile knocking down doors in executive and legislative branches with complaints.

Defining the specific questions you want answered is critical. The overall satisfaction score is a great measure of where things stand, but if you get anything less than superior scores, then you are going to want to know what you can do about it. Is there a specific problem that is pulling down your scores across the board? Or is it a variety of different issues that are hitting stakeholders in different ways? Before the survey is initiated, consider the kinds of questions that will help you take action if you find you have less than satisfied stakeholders.

If you choose to do a survey, you also must be rigorous about analyzing the data and following up with visible actions. You are asking stakeholders to give up their valuable time. They will need to know that this will be a "value add" for them. They should be provided an opportunity to see the overall results, the actions you have committed to take to address issues uncovered, and to witness the changes. A well-run follow-through program is actually one of your greatest opportunities to increase your overall satisfaction scores, because everyone loves to be told they have been heard, what they can expect to see change, and then to see the change happen.

Surveys are best performed by third parties because they allow respondents the opportunity to be anonymous if they choose, although we found that only a very small fraction of those surveyed choose this option. It increases the candor of the comments leading to better insights. Surveys should also offer the opportunity to add comments the survey respondent wants to offer. There is some risk here as personal pet peeves can get aired, but some very valuable insights about why respondents chose to score questions in particular ways can be lost without some room for commentary.

What if there is no money for surveys? First, you should ask yourself what else you are seeking to accomplish and whether that has higher value to you than knowing how the public you serve regards the program you are providing for their benefit. If serving the public interest is the foremost goal, then the top priority should be measuring your success as judged by the public you serve.

But let's assume there *really* is no money. There are two options. First, your frontline people who are dealing with constituents can survey, either formally or informally. A more formal survey will give you more consistency in the questions asked. Second, you can hold regular meetings with representatives of key stakeholders to take the temperature of how things are going.

Here's an example of how a BS approach can lead to specific action. At BPA, our BS pointed out that the success of our strategy required generating key stakeholder support. We concluded that relationship management was as important as program management in terms of providing public service. For that reason, we established account executives whose responsibility it was to see our agency's impacts from an outsider's perspective. This helped address problems such as getting different answers from various parts of our organization, being unable to get an answer at all, or our siloed organization not being able to see the connections between cross-organizational issues.

Our survey results indicated that investing in account executives was a valuable commitment we made in terms of improving satisfaction with our program performance. These folks created the opportunity to build understanding, avoid misunderstandings, and generate timely informal feedback.

Financial

A comprehensive strategy though must also engage the other swim lanes. The financial perspective focuses on assuring that the important dollars-and-cents issues for your agency are defined and measured. In most agencies, this means defining the budget, and managing to budget. This is critically important because of the widespread perception that government agencies are unable to manage to budget. Any budget misses reverberate louder and longer than other mistakes, because it feeds into conventional skepticism about government. Actions such as generating a clean audit opinion or meeting specific spending targets to assure adequate program delivery also fit here. Key measures of agency success as defined by stakeholders are important to include. For example, at BPA goals for rates were a key measure impacting stakeholder satisfaction.

Internal Processes

As a policy-oriented person, the internal processes focus took awhile for me to get my arms around. The internal processes perspective focuses on how the service is delivered. Is the service being provided as efficiently as possible. Are best practices being employed? Is technology being deployed that can help improve service or efficiency? Do you have, or can you get, benchmarking data that will allow a comparison against other similarly situated organizations in the public or private sector?

Internal processes focus recognizes that there are likely many entities that could deliver the service you are delivering. What sets you apart? A challenge here is to think as if your organization is in competition to provide the service. Possibly, there *are* other organizations who argue they could do your job as well or better than you. Or similarly situated organizations that serve other constituencies that can represent competition to be the best.

The expectation outside the public sector is that managing internal processes is something we cannot do well. The fact of the matter is that generally public sector employees are rarely rewarded for implementing operational efficiencies, although frequently chastised for process flaws. The rewards and spotlight in government tend to come for working on policy, rather than operations. There is many a cabinet and sub-cabinet level appointee that came in focused on the weighty policy initiatives they intended to implement, but left having spent considerable time responding to complaints about day-to-day operations that have gone awry.

Creating a culture that emphasizes operational excellence requires leadership. There is something about working inside a large organi-zation, particularly when employees are not directly connected to the public, that creates lethargy about process improvement. I witnessed employees ranting about the service they would receive from a state or local agency, and yet be resistant to applying that same sense of outrage to our own processes. There was a very different mindset about our pro-cesses, with many reasons why things are the way they are, and often a sense of resentment about being asked to consider change. This provided the opportunity to point out that dichotomy, encouraging curiosity whether our actions reflected what we would want if we were outside the agency looking in.

To relate employee's personal experience to organizational needs, in employee meetings I used my own experience working with our local schools as an example. I wanted my kids to have a great education with lots of opportunities, but I also was concerned about the level of my taxes. What I really wanted to see from school-district employees was a concern about both educational performance and efficiency. When I could see that commitment to outcomes, I felt better about what my family was getting for my tax dollars. I purposely picked a service that most employees could relate to. Then I would draw the connection to how we needed to think of ourselves in the same manner as what we want from school district employees.

If we want operational excellence (and increasing respect for the public sector), we will have to drive it internally by creating a strategic focus. Adopting a value like operational excellence is a good first step. Where the rubber begins to hit the road is in defining an operations strategy that prioritizes process improvement actions that will lead to better service to the public because of focused management attention and resources. The internal process swim lane of the BS forces a conversation about what are the highest value internal process actions that will benefit the public.

A well-run organization will have identified and reviewed its core processes to link work products to the strategic plan. That review would also provide for eliminating unnecessary, redundant, or inefficient work. It would also identify processes that can lead to errors.

It can be a daunting task to identify and review all processes. Most organizations only have time and money to pick out some key processes to get started. Choose based on what process improvements would provide the greatest benefit to the public. Usually, this involves some form of interaction with the public. For BPA, it was billing. It's a guaranteed once-a-month interaction with the customer that when errors were made were sure to leave a lasting impression. Nobody wants to pay too much, or be asked to make up underpayments due to an error. Yet, billing was generally a low-profile activity for management. Billing errors undercut our efforts to have customers perceive us as competent to run the business. We had to make a conscious decision to make it a management priority. We did so because of its high-potential benefit to stakeholder satisfaction.

New technology to improve processes is the land of tremendous opportunity and threat in the public sector. It seems well understood across public and private sector organizations that new technology is among the most difficult to predict in terms of budget and schedule planning. New technology also offers the most potential for efficiency improvement. There can, however, be a lot of pain for a public sector organization because divergences from budget and schedule are assumed to be management errors. My belief is that public sector technology projects have to be managed differently than the private sector, with even more emphasis on planning, and less willingness to alter scope even if it adds value, and an intense focus on getting a working model in place within schedule and budget.

People and Culture

Finally, there is the element of people and culture. No organization can be effective if it does not have the right skill set or the right culture. Building design firms would be hard pressed to operate without strong architectural skills, and new start-ups need an entrepreneurial mindset. Public sector organizations need strong skills throughout the organization focused on public service.

This is another area where there are similarities, but also significant differences from the private sector. Engineering, accounting, legal, and economic skills have to be strong in either a private or public sector organization. To get the highest level of performance in government, though, requires a culture that celebrates and focuses on our public service mission. We need to have goals in the people-and-culture swim lane that build on our unique advantage in the public sector. That seeks to enhance pride in our work as public servants.

One can start by establishing the goal of fostering an environment focused on serving the public interest. Having a strategy discussion that includes a focus on the people-and-culture element forces a conversation about actions that will be taken. Here are a few options for potential priority actions:

(1) Establishing the organization's adopted public service-oriented values as criteria for personnel selections. This tends to weed out skill-

competent, but value-deficient candidates, while also sending an important signal as to what values are important to hiring and promotion within the organization. Trustworthiness, for example, could be a core value that is evaluated in the hiring process.

(2) Providing training that encourages subject-matter mastery. A people-and-culture focus on encouraging employee subject-matter mastery builds both pride and competence. An action item could, for example, include a commitment to individual development plans and resources for training for all employees. The plans could be sized to available resources. We need continuous improvement from our employees. Our commitment to grow their skills also builds loyalty to our organization.

A closely related option would be providing training to respond to the dispiriting way the public can sometimes choose to engage with public sector employees.

(3) Celebrating employee success in improving public satisfaction in a manner that can be uplifting for the whole organization. At BPA, we were blessed with a team that went above and beyond to put on an annual event that identified and recognized winners across a variety of categories, including meritorious, value-creating long-term service, courageous acts, and unsung heroes. The recipients were nominated and judged by fellow employees. The awardees and their families were invited to a reception and then an award ceremony broadcast across the complex. Upon receiving their award, their nomination highlights were read and then the awardee was provided a minute at the microphone in what invariably turned out to be a very touching statement. The audience was always large, and the awardees were heartily and loudly cheered.

Smaller organizations, like Chelan, may not be able to afford an effort this large. But less formal programs such as monthly celebrations that feature best examples of taking personal accountability, for example, can be communicated through press releases, internal websites, awards, or small-dollar gifts.

(4) Addressing the challenges of dealing with poor performers. We should also make a strategy choice to deal with poor performers. It can be extraordinarily emotionally difficult and time-consuming work. Yet, I heard a tremendous resentment within the work force at BPA and Chelan about the relatively small number of poor performers. They are

poison in the workforce. A manager dealing with a poor performer can expect it to be emotionally difficult and may feel a lack of management or organizational support. A strategy discussion creates the opportunity to assess a willingness to support managers who are willing to do the hard work of seeking to get improved performance or a change in job status from underperformers. It takes a resource commitment from management and training to support the courageous managers willing to take action. *Talking* about the need to address poor performers is not enough. Management will need to provide human resource, legal, and emotional support to those managers who take on this difficult task.

While performance issues are difficult to tackle, we must remember who we work for. Imagine again that your friends, neighbors, or relatives were watching your activity. Would they believe you are acting in their best interests if you did not have a strategy for recognizing your strong performers that are providing great public service, or for addressing your weak links?

(5) Better connecting our employees on a personal level to the people we serve. When employees can meet or hear directly from the people who benefit or are poorly served by the organization, it enhances their commitment to providing quality service. Creating time for an employee to join a customer conversation to hear the angst of a single mother who was unable to pay the bills turned out to be highly motivating for an entire group that had been struggling with a continuous improvement project.

Conclusion

Clearly defined and communicated mission, vision, values, and agency strategy provides guidance with reach throughout the organization. It helps provide a compass to the individual, like me at the beginning of this chapter, who can miss the big picture in the zeal to make a difference. A Balanced Scorecard provides a structured process to assure implementation is broadly considering key factors for success and focused on the most important activities.

It's time to move to developing a one-year performance plan using your strategic plan outcomes and BS as the guide. This will be discussed in the next chapter.

5

Strategy into Action: Performance Plans

Far better is it to dare mighty things, to win glorious triumphs, even though checkered by failure, then to take rank with those poor spirits who neither enjoy much nor suffer much, because they live in the gray twilight that knows neither victory or defeat.

—Teddy Roosevelt

As a member of the board of directors for many trade associations, I was often apprehensive about doing performance reviews with the executive director. This was mostly the result of one experience in which the executive director had managed to convince the board to shelve the use of a detailed performance plan that included real metrics. Unless there is a detailed performance plan, the discussion becomes a review of the many good things the organization had accomplished over the course of the year, but tied to vague overall strategies. There would often be no discernment of expectations at the beginning of the year to actuals. These exercises were a waste of time, when critical thinking about celebrating success—along with identifying opportunities for improvement— could have occurred. It's good for patting the executive director on the back, which is important in performance reviews, but not for seeking continuous improvement. In addition, there is a lack of documentation to address serious performance issues should they arise.

Whether in the private or public sector, there are many strategy documents gathering dust on shelves. There is one simple action that translates a strategy document into action: Have every senior manager's performance plan derive from the actions on your Balanced Scorecard tied to the strategic plan. The plans have to include metrics that can measure the performance. Then, cascade down the performance plans to individuals throughout the organization. Immediately, the discussion about how the strategic plan gets implemented becomes more relevant. The implementation of the strategy discussion becomes more immediate and apparent.

Using this approach, serving the public interest, defined in terms of mission, vision, and values, is translated into strategy. The strategy is then converted into concrete, measurable actions. It's appropriate at vital times, such as annual performance reviews, to test whether in fact the translation has been successfully accomplished. Are the actions that your organization has committed to ones that ultimately lead to the highest value opportunities for increasing stakeholder satisfaction? The structure should drive this outcome, but any strategic planning process can get sidetracked. A simple test is whether you as a leader will feel proud of and satisfied with what you have accomplished in terms of serving the public interest if your performance plan is successfully implemented.

Performance plans are common in the private and public sector. They establish goals for the organization, sub-organizations, and all the way down to individual employees. This is commonly done in a two-step process: First, establish goals consistent with the period of the strategic plan (at Chelan this was for five years). This creates the architecture. Then, the more critical piece is establishing one-year goals that are designed to drive organizational performance.

There are, however, some elements unique to establishing goals in the public sector. Most important is clear communication between your organizational management and the appropriate governing body regarding the expectation for key goals.

KEY TAKEAWAYS

While public and private sector organizations are benefited by performance plans, there are unique approaches to developing performance plans in the public sector.

Strong governing authority-management relationships can be built through clarity around the level of difficulty assumed in establishing performance plans. The best plans seek high achievement, with an expectation that not all goals will be achieved.

Performance plans translate strategic direction into achievable outcomes. SMART (specific, measurable, attainable, relevant, and time-based) goals tied to the Balanced Scorecard create the greatest clarity between management, governing boards, and the public. It is critical to gain agreement between the governing body and senior management as to what the likelihood of success is for start-of-year goals.

Score organizational performance goals based on objective review whether the result was achieved, not level of effort. Retain the ability to make subjective decisions about the degree of difficulty and level of effort in individual performance reviews.

Performance plan targets create opportunities to strategically address issues that position the organization to serve the public interest. Thought should be given to the outcomes that will best position the organization to create results that will increase public confidence and organizational pride.

The determination as to the number of performance standards and how they will be reviewed in public needs to be based on the goals of management and the governing authority.

Governing authority-management relationship

Public sector organizations should strive to be great. This is what best meets the public's expectation for performance. Striving to be great means setting the bar high for performance expectations. If goals are set high, it should be expected by governing authorities that not all goals will be met. But sometimes, this can create problems when performance goals are reviewed in public session.

Candidly, not all governing officials, especially when elected, are prepared to be understanding when all performance goals arc not mct, even if goals were set assuming nothing goes wrong, and no intervening issues arise. So, the establishment of goals has to be a collaborative discussion about the expectations for percentage of goals likely to be achieved. If the governing officials want a very high percentage, then the goals themselves have to be set with room for the near certainty that issues will arise during the course of the year that cause a need to reprioritize. That translates into setting goals lower and reduces the willingness to take risk. A governing body expectation that performance is 95+ percent achievement of goals translates into management playing it safe.

If the governing authority wants a high percentage and high standards, then performance measures will need to be set with an expectation of regular governing-body engagement in reprioritizing and reestablishing goals throughout the year. This is a time-consuming process that drains energy away from performance that benefits the public.

The best of all worlds is when the governing officials want high performance goals, yet recognize that comes with an expectation that at least some, and possibly many, goals will not be fully achieved. This requires frequent public conversations about goal expectations to assure a high level of trust between a governing body, management, and the public.

The bottom line: governing officials and management need a candid conversation at the beginning of the year about where the performance bar is being set, along with the expectations for performance goals being fully met.

The Difficulty of Translation

Many strategic plans are created without a rigorous review of what it will take to implement the plan. Translation occurs in the subsequent budgeting process. At that moment, the implications of the plan become real. The dollars and staffing needs become obvious, and in many cases, painful. This is an extremely important part of the process where aspirations are confronted with reality. While hard, it is necessary to align expectations with achievability soon after a strategic plan is adopted. SMART goals create clarity at this time. Vague performance goals will only allow misunderstandings about achievable outcomes to persist, leading to difficult rifts between levels of management at end-of-year performance reviews.

Establishing and scoring SMART goals tied to the BS

Clear SMART goals best establish expectations and alignment among all levels of an organization. The biggest benefit comes from the conversations when the goals are being set about what the organization is seeking to accomplish. Written SMART goals force a conversation that reduces the exposure to misunderstandings that only become clear at end of year performance reviews.

A strong Balanced Scorecard tied to the strategic plan creates the organizational focus to assure the strategic plan is being implemented.

"Excellent performance plans align employees throughout the organization on the most important work to serve the public interest."

Let's say there are ten items total in the Balanced Scorecard, across the four swim lanes. Each of these items becomes a section of the performance plan. This assures each of the swim lanes and that key strategic plan elements (which should be included in the swim lanes) are being addressed.

It's hard to set SMART goals. The most common complaint is: *I don't have control over the outcome, so it's not fair to create accountability.* Let's use an extreme example: Say the goal is a legislative outcome that is critical to strategy. A lead government affairs liaison would appropriately assert that they cannot control the legislative branch. That's why it's important to establish goals with an expectation that not all goals will be achieved. What the organization may need is for legislation to be enacted. If that's the case, set the goal to be the outcome that achieves the strategic objective, while recognizing the level of difficulty and control when doing performance evaluations for those employees involved. Be aware, as well, that performance evaluations will always have an element of subjectivity, no matter how SMART the goal may be.

One rule I used for SMART goals: any target that could be accomplished on the first day of the year was unacceptable. For example, any target that begins with words like "Continue to…," "Collaborate with…," or "Work on…" represents goals that with minimal effort can be achieved. These only describe where time will be spent, but not the hard effort of defining the outcome needing to be achieved. The target needs to be difficult to represent the positive and meaningful change we are seeking to accomplish.

Final scoring of performance targets should be based on *yes* or *no*, *green* or *red* as to whether the target was met. In my view, kindness should be applied in the overall individual performance evaluation, but not the scoring of whether an organizational performance target is achieved. "Soft scoring" a SMART goal tends to undermine public confidence in whether the expectations for performance are set high enough. Moreover, public trust is reduced when performance standards are all green at the end of the year due to level of effort, as opposed to results. Its results, not efforts, that the public is seeking out of government.

Soft scoring of results also creates internal dissension because the criteria for evaluation become much more subjective. Your staff will wonder why one part of the organization got a green when the defined target was not achieved, when another one did not. It's a recipe for claims of inequity, and even discrimination. Avoid the pitfalls and judge based on the stated targets.

Identifying key public interests in targets

It's important that key elements necessary for serving the public interest are included as performance targets. For example, if a critical construction project needs to be completed on time and budget to retain public confidence, it should be included as a performance target. If improving relationships with a key constituency is critical, then it's a target. Same with an internal process that needs to be streamlined, or have new technology applied. It's particularly important with respect to the people and culture swim lane. If strengthening understanding and commitment to agency values is important, then it should become a performance target. Or, require development of subject-matter mastery if it is critical to the agency's ability to meet the public's expectations.

Number of Performance Targets and Accountability

There is a legitimate debate about the number of performance targets an organization should manage to. Some believe the number should be small to assure priorities are being set, while creating organizational focus. I prefer a larger set of targets because of the importance of having both the governing board and the public be able to track the issues that are of greatest importance to them. This latter approach also allows more flexibility to alter priorities as circumstances change, because it is less likely to require introducing new targets that have not previously been discussed.

Clear accountability should be established for performance targets. An individual, likely a senior manager, should be identified as the person who has responsibility for managing, tracking, and assuring performance goal attainment or elevating the issue for review.

Public Review

I'm a believer that performance standards should be reviewed in public—and on a regular basis. Done right, this can increase trust between the governing board and management, as well as between the public and the organization. I prefer quarterly reviews, since they allow management to keep the governing authority and stakeholders informed on progress and problems. At the end of the year, goals that are achieved or not achieved are then better understood, since the governing officials and stakeholders are aware of the level of difficulty incurred. Quarterly reports can also identify performance targets that are at risk of not being met (usually marked in yellow), another opportunity for better communication with governing officials and the public. It also engages the public and the governing authority about the potential need for reprioritizing resources.

Utilizing public review does not work for all agencies. Understandably, many national security issues such as cybersecurity protection would be difficult to review in public sessions. Judgment needs to be applied regarding what truly needs to be kept private, as opposed to what is a difficult public conversation, but not compromising to the public interest.

Conclusion

A strong performance plan would have allowed a more meaningful and satisfying performance evaluation with the executive director described at the beginning of this chapter. Course correction opportunities would have been easier to identify. Notable achievements would have been easier to understand, communicate, and celebrate. Excellent performance plans align employees throughout the organization on the most important work to serve the public interest.

Now, we turn to creating a level of accountability necessary for performance plan implementation to be successful.

PART 3

Advancing the Culture

6

Comprehensive Decision Making

I was having a better time at my job than were those of my peers who had opted for private practice. Life as a public servant was more interesting. The work was more challenging. The encouragement and guidance from good mentors was more genuine. And the opportunities to take initiative and to see real results were more frequent..

— Sandra Day O'Connor, US Supreme Court Justice

One day I had a senior manager walk into my office and just unload on me. The manager had been delegated authority to make a decision, but when it was reported out, I had taken issue and ultimately changed the decision. The manager was mostly upset about my lack of trust and undercutting his authority. I was defensive, because I felt the initial decision had insufficient horizontal visibility regarding the effects across the organization. In fact, I remembered becoming increasingly frustrated during the decision meeting with how flawed the manager's initial decision was. I was confident I had appropriately course-corrected, but uneasy because there was merit to the complaint that I had delegated and then second-guessed.

This event, and others like it, led me to the conclusion that delegation involved a lot more than just telling someone they had the authority to make a decision. It was also my responsibility to explain the factors that needed to be considered to make a high-quality decision that would withstand scrutiny.

KEY TAKEAWAYS

It is valuable to have a checklist of the key criteria that should be considered to achieve a high-quality decision. It assures that decision processes at any level within the organization will avoid myopia and *siloing* (focusing only on the interests of one part of the organization). It also helps to ensure that relevant internal expertise is utilized. Clear criteria also allow more effective delegation of decision-making, as the elements for a sustainable decision are defined in advance.

The five factors to consider to make a high-quality decision in the public sector are: financial/operational; legal; environmental; workforce/workplace; and public affairs.

The public affairs or political element of the decision-making process appropriately gets more attention in the public sector because it is testing the strength of connection to serving the public interest.

It is important for any decision maker in the public sector to understand the map of political influence surrounding the issue being debated, and then early on proactively engage those who will most influence the decision.

Avoid process fouls that result in key constituencies being left out.

The public affairs element of a public sector decision may be overwhelmed or underwhelmed in terms of its presence in a decision-meeting. It is up to the leader to create the balance.

Any decision-making process should include an assessment of risk as well as definition of risk mitigation strategies.

The challenges of managing across agency silos are important when creating collaboration and unity for the public. They must be able to perceive their government working to focus first on serving their interests.

Even the best decision-making processes can produce the wrong conclusions. While difficult, be willing to put in place formal and clear resets of policy when necessary to reflect the public interest.

The Risk of Unbalanced Decisions

A classic problem in both governmental and non-government decision making is the unbalanced decision. The unbalanced decision comes from overly focusing on what should be an important, but not the only, factor influencing the decision. It happens because people with delegated authority see the function they have responsibility for, but miss the larger picture of the goals of the organization. It is the result of having tremendous vertical visibility, but lacking horizontal visibility of the impact of the issue at hand. As government and businesses grow larger, this problem becomes more likely.

The flaws in the unbalanced decision only become clear to decision-makers after the policy has been internally elevated, or worse, released. The participants in the decision-making process overlook important elements, not out of malevolence or deceit, but unwittingly.

An unbalanced decision might get the political element correct, but miss on the agency's ability to implement the solution. Or it might be right from a financial/budgetary perspective. but substantially underestimate the legal risk. The bottom line of an unbalanced decision is that there is a high likelihood it will be reversed as it moves up the management chain, as it enters the political arena. or by the courts. A reversed decision represents substantial wasted effort.

This problem can occur for a variety of reasons. Just one individual with a forceful personality in a decision meeting can cause the discussion to become unbalanced. Or an organization can repetitively tend to focus its discussions only on its strength.

Delegation of authority that is not well thought through can create unbalanced solutions as well. Managers are frequently urged to delegate to unleash the power of their organization. But delegation to the lowest levels may leave the delegated decision makers without the view of the horizon the leaders at the top have, leaving important elements of the decision overlooked. Yet, the senior manager remains accountable for the decisions and actions within their organization.

Moreover, organizations are often siloed. It is difficult, even with organizations using a matrixed/shared leadership approach, to avoid one perspective dominating the decision-making process, to the detriment of other perspectives; too often, the organization that was delegated the decision-making authority will lead with what, from their view, seems most important, but does not fully take into account other important factors.. The bottom line is delegation without careful thought can lead to abdication of the responsibility to see across the organizational horizon and ultimately poor decisions. These decisions then must be fixed.

To help overcome this problem at BPA and Chelan, we chose to be clear with our organization about the factors that were important to making a sound decision from an agency perspective. The factors chosen were ones we were confident were relevant to *any* decision. This allowed the organization to prepare analysis within a structure that was necessary for a high quality decision. It also helped ensure that decisions made in the organization with delegated authority would be made with the same scan of the horizon that the leader with statutory authority would use.

The model identified five factors any good decision must address. The five decision factors are not in priority order. In fact, different decisions would place different weights on each of the factors. In some cases, there may be practically no weight on a factor. What is important, though, is that for each decision, the checklist is tested to decide to what extent it should be considered in the decision.

The five factors are:
- What are the financial/operational implications?
- Is it legal?
- Is it environmentally responsible?
- What is the impact on the workforce/workplace?
- What are the public affairs implications?

These five questions are asked in the context of whether the action is consistent with the agency's mission, vision, and values.

Employing a list of decision criteria reduces the risk of myopia in decisions made at any level. It also helps to assure that subject matter expertise within the organization is brought to bear early in the decision process, helping to avoid unwanted surprises later.

It is also important to understand that it is not expected that the decision maker, even when operating with delegated authority, will be an expert in every element of the decision. A benefit of using the decision criteria is to help break down organizational silos. There should be internal expertise available to help evaluate the various decision factors. The check-list helps to assure that internal expertise is utilized.

Financial/Operational

Most decisions have a budgetary impact. Many issues create impacts beyond just whether the money is in the budget or not. What are the costs? Does it create any opportunities for offsetting revenues? Is it allowed within a statutory budget ceiling? A particularly important question, with sometimes counterintuitive answers, is how do the financial impacts land from an accounting standpoint? All of these considerations lead one to want to assure the financial office (or equivalent) is engaged.

There are a set of particularly interesting questions within this realm associated with the risk appetite for an organization. Defining the level of risk appetite and the associated policies should be a collaborative organizational engagement. For example, some organizations will need to address their philosophy as to purchasing decisions about whether the goal is least cost over the long term or low volatility (e.g., variable vs. fixed pricing). These are ultimately decisions that should be decided with input from various parts of the organization, but most importantly decided by governing bodies as to the level of risk the organization is willing to take. The level of risk appetite needs to be matched with financial policies such as level of cash reserves.

Just as important are the operational impacts. How does the decision impact existing operational practices? Will new procedures need to be put in place? Will changes in operational practices impact other agency objectives? A common issue in the hydropower industry is whether a commitment to sell power leading to increased generation would affect fish survival. Without coordination across an organization, these issues could be siloed, leading to less than optimal outcomes.

Legal

A fundamental difference between the private sector and the public sector is that the private sector can take action as long as it is not contrary to law, while the public sector can only take action authorized by law. The onus to assure actions are in accordance with statutory authority is a high and frequently ambiguous bar. Usually the statutes provide general guidance that the policymaker has to interpret with the guidance of counsel. One should not expect to get clear-cut yes-or-no answers on a regular basis as to whether a potential policy is legal. There is subjectivity to interpretation of the law, and as our society becomes more complex that subjectivity in judicial decisions is increasing.

A rule I used with our counsel's office is to provide a percentage in terms of the probability of litigation success on the various elements that were likely to be challenged. This is often difficult for counsel to do. But it is essential to making high-quality decisions. Anything less (e.g., *I think we will win or lose*, or *we have risk of being sustained*) effectively creates an opaque window on an important element of the decision process for the decision maker. When there is no quantitative assessment of legal risk, decision makers have to make their own interpretation of the non-quantitative view. The decision maker should not have to interpret the input of their expert. Instead, seek out your most knowledgeable expert's probabilistic assessment of legal risk.

Environmental Impact

Leaders need to set the tone for how to make often mandatory environmental analysis a vital part of the decision-making process. This will become more necessary over time as the public's commitment to environmental protection grows. But environmental analysis, when used correctly, can be much more than a check-the-box exercise. It can actually be used to improve decision quality.

Just as the public's level of education and information is on an upward trend and inextricably altering the way government must interact with the public, the same is true with environmental protection. It seems clear that the public's willingness and commitment to environmental protection is tied to the collective wealth of the public. The more economically comfortable the public is, the greater environmental protection is desired. Economic downturns will come and go, but the most likely scenario is we will continue to experience long-term economic growth, putting more pressure on the environment, which means we should expect the public's desire for increased environmental protection will also grow. It's such an overwhelmingly important issue to the public that our decisions need to explicitly take it into account.

All major federal decisions and most state decisions require some form of environmental analysis to be performed. Too often, public officials view the environmental analysis process as a threat, particularly to budget and schedule, rather than as an opportunity. Used appropriately, environmental analysis can be a great help to decision makers. Usually, such analysis does not force a particular decision, but it can add substantial understanding of the implications of a decision. It also usually engages a public comment process that, used with transparency, can result in greater public collaboration and buy-in to decisions.

The analysis, which encompasses factors such as socioeconomic analysis as well as impacts to the natural environment, can become a solid foundation for making a high-quality decision. The environmental analysis process usually provides good data. Unfortunately, the process of gathering and coalescing the data can be slow, an area we in government need to improve to make the environmental analysis more useful. If the process takes too long, the data become stale, which can require a costly refresh.

Environmental analysis also provides a venue for engaging the public with a focus on the facts first, rather than emotion. Because it is a formal process, it requires that all comments be addressed and thought through. It engages the public in the choices that are available. It takes time to do it right, but it essentially reflects the understanding that good planning can actually make a project go faster and smoother.

Used inappropriately, in the form of *let's see how fast we can get through this*, environmental analysis can result in costs that are not producing value, slowing necessary outcomes due to failed litigation. It also increases public skepticism of their government because the message is their input is not valued.

Leaders decide how to approach environmental analysis. Is the environmental analysis viewed as a stumbling block that is in the way of making a decision? Or as a tool that can increase public involvement and understanding, as well as the decision-makers' understanding of key variables impacting the decision. When the latter approach is taken, litigation risk should decrease as a result of issues and opinions of the general public being better understood.

The challenge is getting the public to take advantage of the educational opportunity presented in environmental analyses. Too often, commenters only review analyses for points that support their position, or they don't want to hear presentations. Leaders can set the tone when it comes to the intention of public input: it is to better serve the public interest through increasing engagement and understanding, and using the analysis/process to make a more collaborative and informed decision. Leaders can get maximum advantage from the environmental analysis by assuring that the knowledge drawn from public input is included in decision discussions.

"Establish a checklist of key criteria that must be considered to achieve high-quality decisions that avoid myopia and siloing."

Workplace and Workforce

Of the five key decision factors, I have found this is to be the one usually given the least attention, and consequently, it creates the greatest opportunity for error. It was my weakness, since I had more ideas than people to implement.

Changes in policy will require implementation. Can we implement this policy/program in an operationally excellent manner? If we cannot deliver the service in an excellent manner, are we compromising our other activities due to the risk to our reputation? Do we have the number of people we need to be able to implement the policy/program? Do the people here have the skill sets necessary to carry out the functions required? Do we have the tools, including technology, to implement? Are we prepared to make commitments to close any gaps?

Also important, but infrequently considered, is how the activity fits within the organization's culture. If core values have been adopted, is the new activity consistent with those core values? If your core values encompass a public service criteria like being trustworthy, evaluating decisions against that value supports building a public service culture..

This workplace/workforce aspect of the evaluation should also encompass safety risks. Most likely, risks to the public will be covered in your environmental evaluation, but if not this would be the place to do so. But often the risks to your own workforce require a separate evaluation. Do not overlook this element.

Public Affairs

Of the five decision factors, public affairs will get the most focus in this book because of its relevance to the overarching goal of producing stakeholder satisfaction, the measurement of serving the public interest.

Whether one works in the public or private sector, any decision about strategy should include an assessment of the implications for how the public and their elected representatives will react. A good decision anticipates these reactions early in the decision making process.

A useful concept is the political influence map. When confronting an issue that has resonance in the public policy arena, it's valuable to understand where the influence levers are within the political world. A political influence map systematically looks at the sources of external influence that could affect the decision-making process. An experienced decision-maker will have a strategy for early engagement with anyone on the political influence map.

Any lobbyist worth his/her salt and with expertise in a particular area can draw the political influence map once having been told the issue. Moreover, they can also describe the theoretical influence map alongside the actual influence map, given the interests, predilections, relationships, and influence of occupants of various seats of power. To be a successful decision-maker, one must have at least a mental map of where outside influence will seek to be exerted. A decision maker must be able to draw the map to understand which public figures are going to be asked by stakeholders to engage, will likely want to have input to the decision, and to identify who should be strategically engaged early. Otherwise, the decision-makers will constantly find themselves reacting to unanticipated incoming flack from public officials that is probably informed by only one side of an issue.

Due to the checks and balances built into government, there are many sources of power that can influence how decisions get made beyond what would be seen on an hierarchical organization chart. If you want to be successful in the public sector, you must think through the political influence those who are interested in your decision will have. Moreover, if you want to develop a sustainable bipartisan solution as the preferred alternative, then you must have a picture of who are the most crucial actors and how to engage them early and often.

Generally in this book, we are dealing with decisions made within the executive branch. Therefore, the center point of the map and the starting point is the person delegated the authority within the executive branch to make the decision. Usually, the statute will define the position that has the responsibility to make the call, although this may be delegated. The identified decision-maker is responsible for managing the process and more than anyone else must understand the limits to their decision-making authority; they must also be able to draw the political influence map.

Everyone in the executive branch ultimately reports to the chief executive. The delegated decision maker's actions and decisions reflect on the chief executive. The decision maker has to think through how the decisions will reflect the views of the chief executive. It is up to you as a decision maker to reflect the will of the senior elected official in your chain of command, within the confines of the law, assuming they have all the facts that you do. In fact, you have to be prepared for the likelihood that your decisions will be tested by constituents and their lobbyists, appealing on the basis that a decision does not reflect the views of the chief executive on process and/or substance.

I certainly had many of my decisions tested up my management chain. It's difficult to keep senior administration officials informed of all the things going that they may be asked about. But, because its hard is a bad excuse for not finding ways to make it happen. Sometimes you have to just keep sending out information, even when there is no immediate response.

You also have to be prepared for the linkage to a major issue that the chief executive is working on, but which is ancillary to your responsibilities.. A philosophical approach to a large issue may spill over to your situation-specific concern. I'm reminded of national debates over electricity policy that impacted decisions on specific transmission projects. Frequently, the only way to identify these linkages is to perform outreach to the boss, or likely, key influentials in the process.

Decision-makers also have to think through how the issue will be presented to the chief executive. For example, let's say you have the responsibility to manage a decision process, or advise a decision maker on a decision process that is certain to generate substantial controversy. You would want to think through what issues will be critically important to constituents and how they would present them to your more senior officials. For any even modestly controversial issue, it can be assumed that constituents or their lobbyists will seek to engage more senior officials. Usually this is on the basis that their policy views are being ignored down the chain. And undoubtedly, there will be examples where the chief executive has expressed support for a principle, either privately or publicly, that supports what the constituent wants.

Obviously, the influence map should include lines to all the people up the decision maker's management chain to the highest level that access may be granted.

A more challenging piece to evaluate for inclusion on the influence map are the influentials within the executive branch that are not in the direct chain of command. On any given issue there are senior leaders at other federal agencies that have related policy responsibility. There are also advisors to the chief executive with related policy experience (e.g., at the Office of Management and Budget, National Security Council, Council on Environmental Quality). These are targets for outside parties to try to engage in the policy process. After years of watching this, I must admit to finding it humorous when an agency official with delegated decision-making authority would be surprised and offended when an end-run outside the direct management chain would be attempted. Of course that is going to happen. Leaders should expect and anticipate that it will happen. Potential key influentials who are not in the direct management chain should be on the influence map, with a related strategy for engagement that precedes contact by outside influences.

The second key area to consider is the legislative branch. Is there a state or Congressional district that is especially impacted by the policy at hand? If so, you can be fairly certain the representative for that area is going to be asked to weigh in and need to be engaged early. Is this an issue that will rise to the level of engagement by the authorizing or appropriations committees with relevant jurisdiction? If so, again it's your job to make sure they have the full picture of what is at stake early in the process.

The delegated decision maker (and their advisors) job is to see the playing field and understand that controversial issues will be debated across the public arena. Anticipate where it will go and engage the key officials and their staff.

Moving early

The concrete is drying. One of my most influential mentors frequently used that saying when a new issue was forming . What he meant is that in the public policy arena, it's important to define the issue early.

Waiting to visit key influencers until after others have gotten there first means dealing with at least partially dry concrete. It's harder to mold when chipping, rather than smoothing.

Putting the problem in full context for key influencers is much easier when the concrete is still wet. Since they are often public figures, constantly in the spotlight and asked to take positions on emerging issues, once they have taken a public position on an issue it is much harder to get them to be open-minded about the policy at hand.

It's part of our culture to denigrate *flip-flopping* on issues, something I have always found curious. In fact, we tend to compliment people who are continuous learners and willing to change their views based on new information. Not so, though, in the political arena. We have trained our politicians to be resistant to altering a position once taken, even when the initial position was based on bad information.

Hence, we need to move quickly when trying to manage an issue to assure that public figures can see the whole picture, and what's at stake— before the concrete has dried. Assuring the problem is seen in full context by public figures is much easier when the concrete is still wet.

I used to keep a concrete brick on my desk as a reminder of the absolute necessity of being pro-active in the public policy arena. I made sure that all the key political influentials could see the horizon of public policy issues that were in play so that they were not taking positions on limited information.

There is another key benefit to being pro-active and engaging political influentials early: Senior political officials greatly appreciate seeing the full array of aspects associated with a decision, and knowing that you are taking their perspective into account. Bring people into the discussion by telling them all the things that you can see that seem relevant to the decision, then ask what they can add to that. You can get some powerful insights. And you are building collaboration.

Once the map of influential elected officials and their representatives is complete, the next question is, *who influences the influencers?* For a member of Congress, which constituent group is most likely to be listened to? What media (social or traditional) is likely to influence the thinking? A robust influence map sees all the figures who are likely to influence the process and connects to the grassroots actors that are likely to play a role. Once again, it is important to be proactive and seek to get to these parties early if you want the debate in the public arena to be informed and comprehensive.

This process starts from the person with the statutory or delegated authority to make the decision. It goes up with solid lines within the hierarchy of the executive branch. But executive branches are big, and there are influentials that operate as key advisors to the solid-line officials. In the federal government, many issues have to be resolved below the level of the President. A large set of organizations provide filters for decision making that, if not adroitly engaged, can alter, slow, or even halt decision making. These include the Office of Management and Budget, the National Security Council, and the Council on Environmental Quality. Within each are key advisors who when engaged early can become helpful collaborators and allies, and who when engaged late can be key stumbling blocks. These organizations are usually connected with dotted lines, although at times they can become solid lines if the issue is important enough and has multiple cabinet-level agencies involved.

Legislators also receive dotted lines because they are not in the chain of command, yet they can have significant influence on the process. If the issue becomes big enough, they can become controlling through statutory changes. Finally, there is the connection to key constituencies that will influence all of the elected officials and their representatives in the process.

Drawing the political map may seem intuitive and unnecessary to seasoned political veterans. The map serves three purposes, however:

First, a systematic review often uncovers blind spots. Putting it on paper requires thinking it through carefully.

Second, it helps the people who will be working on the project who likely do not have the same level of political expertise. It is important to have your troops understand what factors are influencing the decision, and how impacted parties are being engaged. It helps them to see the full playing field of public interests.

Third, the drawing of the map should be a collaborative effort within your organization, bringing in your external affairs experts and your program experts who best understand stakeholders' views. This effort helps to create a greater sense of team among these different elements of your organization.

Avoiding process fouls

When considering how to engage actors on the political influence map, think about what complaints are likely to be made. Complaints about a decision will generally fall into the categories of process and substance.

Process issues, if unattended, are the easiest for those outside the direct decision making chain to engage. Process fouls usually result from a lack of attentiveness to a key constituency. They allow a key influential (e.g., a legislative branch official) to engage on behalf of a constituent without necessarily taking a position that will make other constituents unhappy. Rectifying process errors can go all the way to having to start from the beginning.

When dealing with a controversial subject, it is practically inevitable that those aggrieved by a decision will object to both the substance and the process. The best defense against a process charge is to anticipate these challenges and run a process that creates opportunity for all voices to be heard and addressed. Even if it extends the timeline. Overall, this level of transparency is most consistent with how to best serve the public interest. And from my experience, seasoned elected officials will give more deference to a well-run process that does not feel like it was biased against a particular set of interests.

The substance issues are your agency's expertise. I have only two important points: First, you must be able to explain the substance issues to all constituents concisely and accurately (see Chapter 11). Second, stay alert to the issues dominating the headlines; your issue could be placed in the larger context of whatever is currently in the public spotlight (e.g., jobs, taxes, national security, etc.) and expectations change, accordingly.

Discussing politics in internal decision meetings

In my view, politics is generally not a dirty word. Engaging the views of elected officials is the appropriate vehicle to assure democracy is being implemented. In this light, a discussion of the political element is a necessary component of any sound decision making process in the public sector. As a general rule, it should get more discussion in the public sector than in a private sector organization.

While discussions of public affairs inside a public sector agency are appropriate, too often they either error on the side of excess or ignorance, each of which causes its own problems. Here are examples of the kinds of statements that get made after meetings when the political issues either dominate or get buried:

Those guys don't have a clue about the politics and they are going to get killed when this goes out.

There was no substance to that meeting. It was just a bunch of political animals strutting around. The policy will fail and they don't even see it coming because they don't understand how it works.

Anyone who has spent an extended period of time in the public sector is likely to have heard comments that resemble these. If you choose to work in the public sector, it should not come as a surprise that politics will need to be a part of the decision process. It can be so alluring, though, that it takes all the airtime. Alternatively, and often in response to meetings that are all about the politics, a decision discussion will occur that ignores how the policy will land in the public arena.

I have heard both these comments, and many variations, coming out of meetings. The commenter was usually right. These were failed meetings. They failed because the leader did not manage the time and agenda to allow an appropriate discussion of each of the five decision factors.

Here is an example of a fictitious internal decision meeting. In this case let's use the potential for implementing a tax on carbon emissions:

Most economists would assert that a carbon tax would create the most economically efficient outcome in terms of achieving carbon emission reductions. Yet, as a country we have consistently chosen less efficient means. An extended discussion of a carbon tax that does not include a discussion of how to address the political challenges constitutes mental recess.

But there are times when participants in decision meetings on key public policy issues choose to assert that they are "above politics," seeking to ignore the subject altogether. This may be appropriate in a brainstorming phase, but not when real decisions need to be made. When operating in the public arena, a group charged with making a decision must understand the political paths opponents would take to block or overturn the decision.

We must also understand how a policy will be portrayed, depending on the position of the opposition. Going back to the example of a carbon tax, it would likely be portrayed as simply "a tax" that will fund all government activities, no matter what promises are made. The alternative policies for carbon emission reductions in almost all cases result in higher costs for consumers per unit of carbon emissions reductions. Yet, these costs do not come with the label of a tax. Hence, the alternatives are more acceptable in a democracy where people's reactions and votes matter. Debating the issue of a carbon tax without considering the politics involved is a waste of valuable time. It may be appropriate to try to change the political perspective through facts and education, but it would be folly to ignore the political landing zone.

On the other hand, a debate that only considers the political implications of a subject threatens to overlook the fundamental policy objectives and how to make government work. Key issues like: *what are we trying to accomplish, how do we achieve that goal cost-effectively,* and *what will it take to implement the policy including money and people?*

Decision makers need external affairs experts in the room who can explain how a policy will land in the political arena. They also need people who know how to make the operational aspects of government work. Unfortunately, the gap between these two sets of experts tends to be vast. Only a few people bridge this gap in their careers. It is not unlike businesses, which have planners and implementers. Implementers tend to complain that the planners do not live in the real world and that the plans have to be constantly modified to have a chance of succeeding. Planners tend to complain that the implementers are messing up their carefully orchestrated concepts. Similarly, political and operational professionals have to participate simultaneously to achieve good and feasible public policy.

A critical role for the person running a decision meeting is to assure that both these points of view get adequate time to raise and address their issues, but that neither dominates. If you want to lead in the public sector, you must plant your feet in the worlds of political professionals and program experts. You must have comprehension of the political dynamics at play, and critically, you must be able to draw the map of political forces that will be at work on the issue leading up to the key decision maker. Yet, you must also understand factors such as resource availability that can lead to a poorly implemented policy.

The ramifications of a poorly implemented policy, once pointed out, are usually clear to your political pros. For example, investigations by auditors like the Government Accountability Office or Inspector General, hearings before legislative bodies, and media attention on poorly implemented programs all cut into an agency's political capital. Usually, reminders of these outcomes are enough to cause the political pros to realize it is worthwhile to spend time on thinking through the implementation up front, even if it is boring to them. Similarly, the ramifications of a poorly designed policy without political awareness, once pointed out, are usually clear to implementation professionals.

Doing a bunch of work and having it become trashed in the political arena is both a waste of resources and demoralizing.

A successful leader, at whatever level in the organization, needs to point out the futility of choosing to focus the discussion on only some elements necessary for a high-quality decision. The goal is to make sure the reaction of participants after a decision meeting does not mirror the statements earlier in this chapter.

Risk Assessment and Mitigation

The evaluation of each of these five main factors—financial/operational, legal, environmental, workforce/workplace, and public affairs—results in assessment that in most cases is not clear-cut, but instead tends to identify areas of risk. As staff are engaging the evaluation, it is important to acknowledge this is likely to happen. Embrace the identification of risks, and even more important, potential risk mitigation. Don't count on everything going well. Be prepared for the biggest risks by taking protective or mitigation actions. This takes time and money, but it substantially increases the odds of a successful outcome to the decision process.

Cross-Agency Siloing Issues

Special attention needs to be called to one of the most vexing problems associated with government decision making, one that gets more problematic the larger the governmental body. This challenge is particularly evident in the federal government: how to get federal agencies working on a common problem to work collaboratively, to avoid fighting with each other in public, and to avoid having even minor issues being elevated to an executive level for resolution.

This is an issue tied to delegation of authority, but on a much grander scale because of the size of government. The challenge is made even greater when, as happens frequently, the coordination must occur between agencies that ultimately report to different cabinet-level positions. Establishing a group at a level above all agencies within a governmental structure (the White House level for the federal government) with both depth of knowledge and time to resolve issues is, at best, cumbersome.

A workable solution to managing issues that have cross-agency implications is one of the most critical issues confronting anyone committed to making government work better for the people. It is very easy for agencies to get caught up in carrying out their statutorily authorized responsibilities, yet lose sight of how the government as a whole is impacting the public we serve.

Positions get taken at the first level of engagement between agencies that promote their own responsibilities, but not with a government-wide perspective. As that position gets elevated, it is described in terms of what is at stake for the individual agency's authority, rather than what is at stake for the public. This results in agencies going toe-to-toe at senior levels, mostly because the participants have an opaque view of the entire impact on the public.

I have witnessed this scenario repeatedly. It is one of the most frustrating issues confronting senior leaders in the executive branch. It leads to slow, and often poor, decision-making. It leads to agencies working as part of the same executive branch arguing with each other in public. It leads to dismay on the part of the public as to how disorganized the government seems to be, and questions about who is in charge. It reflects poorly on the chief executive and their most senior leadership.

More meetings of senior level executives in the executive branch might help solve this problem if the participants had the time for the meetings, and to prepare for refereeing the disputes. Seldom is that true. But there is a better way.

In the Northwest, we struggle with addressing the needs of salmon and steelhead in the Columbia River Basin listed under the Endangered Species Act (ESA). These are iconic animals whose existence is important to many people, most of all the Native American salmon tribes.

The responsibility for ESA management of salmon rests with the Fisheries Division of the National Oceanic and Atmospheric Administration (NOAA-Fisheries), itself a part of the Department of Commerce. The fish traverse the main stem of the Columbia and Snake Rivers, where there are a series of dams that provide navigation, irrigation, flood control, recreation, and electric power production benefits. The Army Corps of Engineers (part of the Department of Defense) and the Bureau of Reclamation (Interior) operate the dams. BPA (Energy) markets electric power from them, producing a revenue source that repays a substantial portion of the construction and operation costs of the dams. The Fish and Wildlife Service (Interior) manages hatcheries used to mitigate for damage caused by dams to fisheries. The Environmental Protection Agency tracks water quality.

The National Park Service (Interior) manages recreation sites at the dams. And on it goes, including (very importantly) the Department of Justice which represents all the federal agencies in the courtroom.

While the responsibility under ESA rests with NOAA-Fisheries, there are many steps in the process of deciding how to list and protect endangered and threatened species. Each of the agencies listed above has points in the process where it has the lead for producing products (e.g., decision documents, press releases, etc.) that will enter the public consciousness.

In the 1990s, a desire to manage policy on this significant issue, combined with unresolved disputes between the agencies, led to the engagement of the White House. Here is where unresolved policy issues come to be decided in the unitary executive. In this case, the matter was put in the hands of the chairman of the Council of Environmental Quality (CEQ), who is the president's point person on environmental issues.

The challenge of managing the Columbia Basin salmonid issues at that high a level proved to be daunting. The river never stops running downhill, and hence, the array of issues affecting how the river should be operated under constantly changing flow and temperature, as well as juvenile and adult migration conditions, proved daunting. The solution that evolved was the formation of set of teams beginning at the White House level and cascading down to the regional level.

The formation of the teams was the easy part. The difficult part was creating a culture that was based on collaboration and problem solving at the lowest possible level. That happens best when there is a leadership commitment and role modeling to seek collaborative solutions.

The structure for this approach was formalized in a Memorandum of Agreement (MOA) that established a caucus of federal agencies with responsibilities for managing salmon in the Columbia River Basin. Its purpose was to resolve issues in the region as much as possible. The need for such an approach was nonpartisan: the federal caucus was initiated in the Clinton administration, and continued in the Bush and the Obama administrations.

The MOA does *not* speak to many of the key issues necessary for an effort like this to be successful. It does *not* speak to collaboration, and only speaks to decision-making in obligatory clauses that retain each agency's statutory decision-making authority. It does, however, include one key clause that establishes the framework for respectful collaboration between the agencies: It requires (without penalty for noncompliance) that the agencies exercise a policy of *no surprises* with respect to public pronouncements.

It turns out that the adoption of such a policy is quite powerful. It leads to sharing information in advance of release. The sharing allows potential conflicts to be identified, resolved, or elevated as necessary, including how an action today by one agency may impact the future action of another agency. The result is more holistic and strategic decisions. Ultimately, this simple rule provided the foundation for building a cross-agency integrated team focused on the impacts of decisions to the public.

The sharing philosophy was enforced only through peer pressure. It was combined with a commitment from leadership to act in a collaborative manner to avoid elevating any but the most critical matters that made the peer pressure more effective.

The delegation to the regional federal caucus did not represent delegation with abdication. Columbia Basin salmon issues are a highly visible issue on the political screen, attracting media attention and frequent requests from constituents to meet with the highest levels of government, along with regular interaction with members of Congress. The participants understood that work products would need to be consistent with the philosophy of the president. Key decisions would need to be blessed by senior political officials. Any unresolved disputes would be elevated.

Over time there was an evolution of two criteria by which the federal caucus' work was measured: Any plan should support the environmental and economic health of the region. Any plan should also be scientifically credible, legally defensible, and politically sustainable. In effect, these were the decision criteria.

People on both sides of the issue will argue that the policy conclusions have been imperfect: the government is not doing enough for salmon, or, the government's actions for salmon cost too much. The purpose of this section is not to argue the policy merits, which only time will tell as to how well they work. What *is* clear is that on a divisive issue which engaged multiple federal agencies, a process was adopted that resulted in plans that were implemented across two quite different administrations with broad, although not unanimous, bipartisan congressional support. It generated a plan under the Bush Administration that underwent significant scrutiny from the Obama Administration.

That review resulted in modifications reflecting the view of a need to do more to manage risk to the species, but not a rewrite of the program. This was remarkable given the significant differences in philosophy between the two administrations on environmental/economic issues.

A simple, relatively informal management structure like this can be very powerful. For it to generate conclusions that have government-wide support, without the sniping along the way, it takes a commitment of the senior federal agency officials to engage as necessary throughout the process, to push issues down as much as possible, but with clear guidance about what is expected. It also takes a sense of teamwork that must develop at a sub-cabinet level, where each agency's needs for serving the public are being understood and addressed in an holistic fashion.

The federal employees at all organizational levels who participated in this process described it as among the most meaningful and rewarding experiences in their career. The issues addressed were controversial and difficult, meaning tension was a regular part of the process. But over time, there became an overarching desire to be successful at finding solutions that met the various statutory requirements, as well as creating a plan that would generate bipartisan support.

The feedback the group received from senior leaders in the executive branch was both tough review of the federal caucus recommendations (due to the level of controversy around the issue) and commendation for finding a collaborative approach within the federal family. All too often, senior leaders feel it becomes their responsibility to *manage the squabbling children* in the federal family. An approach that focuses on defining workable solutions that consider all the angles of a problem reduces the burden on senior leaders.

Cross-agency disputes within large governments are not inevitable. The use of criteria for how decisions will be made (in this example through *no surprises* and a commitment to collaboration) with high-level decision criteria can avoid the disarray that undermines the public's confidence in its government. It also takes leadership at various levels of government committed to seeing the larger picture of making the government work to serve the people.

Willingness to Consider a Reset

Let's assume your organization has run an excellent decision process and is now implementing the conclusion. But it's not going well. Despite the best efforts to anticipate relevant issues, surprises have arisen. Stakeholders are reacting more negatively than expected. One of the hardest calls for a leader is when to acknowledge the original guidance was flawed. It seems like an admission of a mistake, and weakness. Frequent changes in direction can undermine the effectiveness of a leader. There are times, though, that more than a minor course correction is necessary.

I can recall a time at BPA, for example when we did not adequately understand the authority of another governmental agency at the time when direction was set. We were getting into a larger morass by pushing forward. We needed to reset the direction.

Resets are difficult to accomplish, however, because organizations once in motion, like ships, require hard steering to redirect. In those situations, my preference was to call the team together, not sugarcoat the situation, and be clear that was time to do a reset of strategy. When this is the decision, leave no doubt in the organization, because otherwise those that have been fighting to accomplish the original mission may not pick up the nuance. Resetting the strategy can be both upsetting and a relief to employees. What makes it harder is if the course correction is only accomplished slowly and sporadically.

Conclusion

The manager at the beginning of this chapter was right to be frustrated, because I had not provided clear guidance at the beginning of the project. I needed to learn that delegating authority came with an obligation to explain the need for horizontal decision making utilizing the relevant criteria for making good decisions. Once that could be articulated, the number of managers expressing frustration with undermined delegated authority declined. Moreover, it taught employees throughout the organization how to think at an executive level, increasing the organizational strength for succession planning. It reduced workload due to rework of sending recommendations back. Internally, it created more satisfaction for everyone involved in making key decisions. Most important, it made for better public policy.

7

Accountability as the Catalyst

To complaints of 'poorly done,' one often hears the excuse 'I am not responsible.' I believe that is literally correct. The man who takes such a stand is not responsible; he is irresponsible.

—Admiral Hyman Rickover

When things go wrong in your command, start searching in increasingly larger circles around your own desk.

—General Bruce Clarke

One beautiful day I was eating lunch at a sidewalk café in Washington, DC. I got a call that one of our helicopters, working on a transmission construction project, had gone down and the pilot had been killed. I will never forget the kick-in-the-gut feeling, recognizing that this had happened on my watch. I learned then that no matter what else happens, an on-the-job fatality is the worst day for an organizational leader.

I attended and spoke at the wake a few days later, meeting the pilot's wife, family, friends, and co-workers. There are no words that are sufficient in that moment. I promised we would get to the bottom of the incident and learn from it. That is a solemn pledge. The experience of witnessing the survivor's pain became highly motivational for all our senior leaders.

A root cause analysis (RCA) was conducted with a commitment by our organization's leaders that it would be thorough. During that time, I met with safety experts from outside our agency to get their sense of actions I should take. I must admit that the search for the root cause seemed somewhat distant to me. After all, I was 2500 miles away when the helicopter went down. There were at least four layers of management between the working crew and me. It did not really cross my mind that there would be issues relating to my actions.

The RCA identified about a half dozen errors, any one of which by itself did not cause the accident, but which if corrected might have avoided the accident. If I had just read the report, I might have missed the larger learning. From the safety experts themselves, I heard one clear message: *Safety is a culture that starts at the top.* Leaders must be visible and relentless with the safety message. This is especially true with any routine, yet dangerous, activity that is undergone on a regular basis. The cumulative result of many relatively small independent problems we experienced suggested that the overarching issue was with safety culture. As the organizational leader, that was my responsibility. I was ultimately accountable.

KEY TAKEAWAYS

Increasing personal accountability in your organization is both challenging and critical to effectuating your commitment to public service. We are responsible to the public and must embed that philosophy across the organization.

Use the "ladder of accountability" to explain what it means to take personal accountability. Use the ladder of accountability as a foundation to test reactions and decisions about whether we are acting as victims or acting on what we can control.

Don't allow the use of the term accountability to be limited to addressing poor performers. It is as much about celebrating and learning from success.

Consider describing accountability in four ways that are stages in project management: accountable for defining the vision; bestowing the honor; managing for results; pride and prejudice.

To drive personal accountability into an organization, a leader must be willing to accept responsibility—including for cultural and/or systemic issues—and constantly seek opportunities for self-improvement. If you want continuous improvement, you have to model and drive personal accountability.

The last stage of a project is the most critical for driving accountability. Commit to doing *root cause analysis* and *lessons learned*. Extend the value of this work through thoughtful transparency.

Ban the use of the phrase *good enough for government work*, or similar terms that accept the denigration of standards for high-quality government work.

Put in place four systems-based approaches that address performance management challenges up to and including termination, when warranted: engage human resources and general counsel to encourage and guide supervisors; train supervisors; support supervisors who take on difficult personnel challenges; commit your own time.

The Challenge of Creating Accountability

Establishing a systemic structure based on serving the public interest as the organizing principle is essential. Structure alone, though, will not fully tap into the power of serving the public interest. As in any successful enterprise, increasing personal accountability is necessary to producing results in the public sector. There are, however, unique aspects of working in the public sector that create challenges to this:

First, there is the problem discussed previously: the definition of success is amorphous in the public sector. Pinning down what serves the public interest is difficult. Yet, as discussed earlier regarding performance planning, it can be defined in measurable ways that leads to creating clear accountability. That is our job as leaders. Without that definition and clear assignment of responsibility, we most likely will get performance that does not meet the standards for public service we desire.

Second, even the word "accountability" tends to carry a negative connotation, as in: *I am going to hold you accountable for what you have done wrong.* Many people hear it as a euphemism for *heads are gonna roll.* We need to change that paradigm to focus on a commitment to earning and accepting responsibility.

Third, working in the public sector can be debilitating because it feels too big to manage. We all want control in our lives, but the public sector can be viewed as the black hole of *shared responsibility*—which too often translates into no accountability.

Accountability starts at the top and must be modeled to be successful. Telling staff they need to exhibit personal accountability without embracing it as a personal value is worse than doing nothing at all. This can be especially difficult in the public sector due to the visibility of public sector work.

The Ladder of Accountability

BPA staff introduced me to the most powerful tool I have encountered for encouraging taking personal accountability in a positive way. The ladder of accountability is a simple way to engage in conversation with anyone about how they are addressing a management challenge (or another work issue, or even life outside of work).

A brief explanation of the ladder: At the bottom are victim behaviors, all the way down to being unaware or unconscious. These are easy to recognize, especially if things are not going right. At the top is where we want to be, with accountable behaviors, but it can be difficult under stress to exhibit these characteristics. It's a natural human reaction when there is trouble to blame others. It takes conscious effort to move to behaviors representing what you can control, and then make it happen.

We printed copies of the ladder at BPA, posting them in the hallways. I kept one on the wall in my office. It was a good reminder to myself about how I wanted to act. It was also a good tool to stop a conversation not going well, and check in about where we all were on the ladder in that moment.

What do we want accountability to mean?

Moving away from a negative view of accountability requires effort to define what it means in your workplace. The key is to treat *being given accountability* like the honor it is. I think of this taking place in four distinct steps. These are basic steps that should be part of any good project management approach:

First, a leader, of whatever size group, defines the goal. What is it that we are trying to accomplish that advances the mission, vision, and values of this agency—and will be widely regarded as serving the public

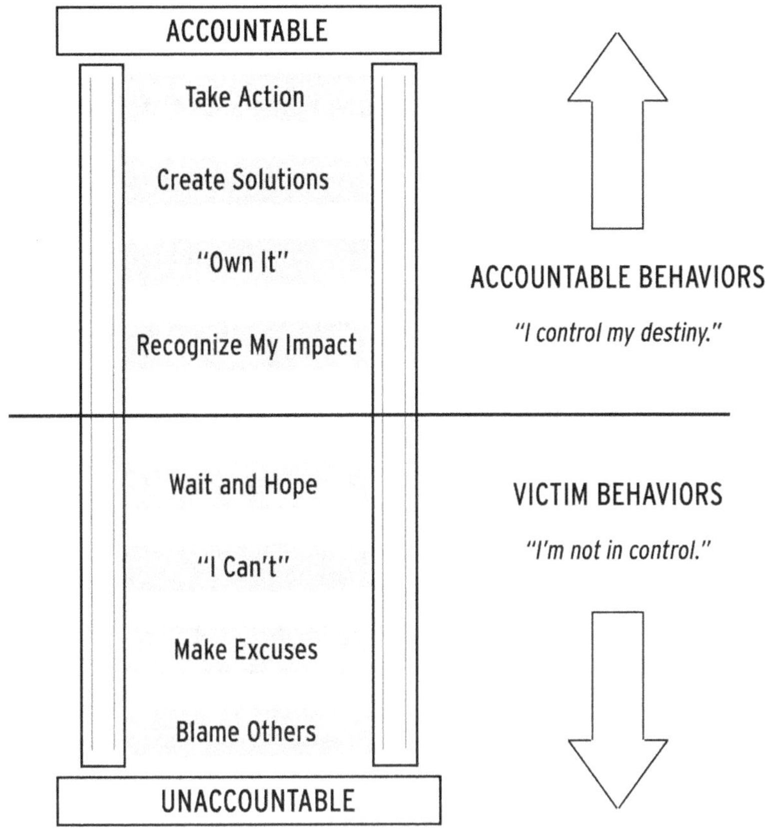

interest? How are we, even if only in some small way, going to make the world a better place? For example, how will we deliver more of this service at a lesser cost than what we do today? Or, how will we improve our stakeholder satisfaction with the process we run? It takes vision. Leaders should be chosen who display an ability to define and articulate a drive for implementing change that helps to make things work better for the benefit of the public. The accountability for developing and advancing the vision rests with the leader.

Let's use as an example one of the most significant issues any agency can face. Agencies with challenges managing to budget have a foundational risk to stakeholder satisfaction. It has to be solved to establish credibility. A leader has to establish the budget management goal, create clarity about the budget target, and the focus on the importance of fixing the problem.

Step two is to bestow the honors. The vision must be translated into a project, and the project probably has multiple steps. The project should be divided into products for which individuals, as parts of teams or not, can be bestowed the honor of accountability. And at this stage of the project, it usually is an honor. Most often, there are people who either overtly or covertly covet being granted the responsibility for delivering various project elements. When they are given the accountability, it should be with fanfare and recognition. This is a moment when there is the opportunity to create and take advantage of personal pride as a motivating force. It should be clear that the project is important and needs their skills to push it to successful conclusion.

Goals and milestones need to be established at the beginning of the project, as well. Clear definition of what constitutes success—by when and at what cost. Goals should represent a horizontal view of what is necessary for agency success. Using the budget example, personal accountability needs to be established line item by line item to assure a single person is accountable for managing each element.

Third is the hard work of managing the project. Accountability must be visible for interim assessments throughout the year (quarterly, monthly, or weekly), depending on the importance of the goal. That means the accountable person will be responsible for making a determination on a regular basis, which is communicated upward (often in the form of a green, yellow, or red signal). For example, those accountable need to determine if the budget commitment is on target to be met by some predetermined time frame (usually, end of year).

A mistake I have made is what I call *watching too gently*: seeing a project appear to not be doing well, and not probing deeply enough due to avoiding being hard on people. The correct answer every time: It is the public's money and you are accountable for assuring dollars are wisely spent. This is not the time for putting people's feelings first. Your primary responsibility is to assure the public's work is being accomplished efficiently. This can be accomplished in a respectful manner toward employees, but it has to be firm with a focus on the primary goal being serving the public interest. Back to our example, line-item budgets needs to be reviewed regularly with a simple system of red, green, yellow, or red to indicate the likelihood of meeting the target.

ACCOUNTABILITY AS THE CATALYST

The final stage is what I call pride and prejudice. This is the area that in my experience tends to be performed in the weakest way within government. In the public sector, we are not very good at acknowledging and rewarding strong performance. When things go really right, our financial tools to reward people are stingy compared against the private sector. For the most part, we are left with using small or non-financial tools. Yet non-monetary recognition can be very effective with many employees who want to know their work is appreciated. Don't make my mistake. I was too often guilty of taking production of results for granted, instead of showering praise and recognition.

Similarly, we tend to want to look away from the car wrecks of program/project management. We don't want to hurt people's feelings and we feel limited in our ability to create consequences for negative performance. We worry about the spotlight of political reaction.

We, however, have tools. I found employees practically universally respond to performance reviews even with small or no financial rewards. The difference between "meets expectation" versus "highly successful" ratings can be highly motivational. In addition, our limited awards dollars can be targeted at rewarding strong performance with remarkable results. There are many forms of non-monetary recognition that are motivational, such as acknowledgement at high visibility events. We have to make an effort to use these tools.

Another tool that we vastly underestimate is the capability of transparency to motivate performance. A culture of transparency around scoring organizational performance plans can be powerfully motivating, even if we have limited positive or negative consequence tools. Commit to performing *lessons learned* and *root cause analysis* on all projects, whether they are perceived as successful or not. With this process, high performers are recognized. It also allows projects that have underperformed to be analyzed in a visible way, focused on how the project could have been led differently.

Nearly all projects have elements that have gone exceedingly well and those that have not. Lessons learned about what went right are as valuable to the rest of the organization as what went wrong. Moreover, it's less threatening to project participants when both what went right as well as what went wrong are highlighted. Where problems are identified, use a root cause methodology (there are many) to assess what led to the problems, with a commitment to address issues that are uncovered.

Where will the finger point?

Now you must be prepared for something that is very hard. There is a high likelihood a portion of the problem uncovered will point back to you. The leader establishes the culture and the culture may have contributed to the success or failure of a project. Or an early decision you made set the context for the project. Take a risk. Embrace the opportunity to learn and get better. Be a role model for your people that transparency will help you and your agency get better at providing public service.

Being responsible for everything is both one of the great joys and great burdens of leadership. There is the excitement about being responsible for important, meaningful decisions. Then there is being accountable when things don't go right.

My experience with RCA and lessons learned is that most of the time there is something I as a leader could have done and should be doing to prevent the identified problem from occurring again. It may have to do with the organizational culture. Or it may have to do with systemic issues that reach beyond individual incidents.

If you believe your people are letting you down, they may be, but you are probably contributing to the problem in some way through the way you are avoiding taking accountability. Culture and systems are the leader's responsibility. Be prepared to own at least a piece of the problem, or else you are likely a part of the ongoing problem.

Taking accountability personally

It is hard, but choose to be willing to self-examine in a meaningful way and then act on what you have learned. Your instincts will be to deny responsibility. Resist these urges and plunge in no matter how difficult. You can point the finger of blame at others, but ultimately you are accountable, and you only undercut your own future effectiveness when you suggest it's all someone else's fault. You owe it to your employees to set the right example. You owe it to the public you are committed to serve.

With respect to the safety issue that arose from the fatal helicopter accident, I chose an extremely difficult, but very powerful course. I heard from safety experts it was up to me to establish the safety culture. I needed to take action to improve the culture. At safety meetings, I would ask participants to imagine what it would be like to tell a loved one of a co-worker that the person had died or been severely injured on the job. We'd pause for three minutes to reflect on what that would feel like. Then I would relate what it had been like to speak at the funeral of an employee who had died on the job. I could never get through that without an emotional upwelling.

I would share that I was accountable for everything that happened at BPA (and later, Chelan) including establishing the safety culture. My commitment was to do whatever I could to establish safety as a priority for our organization, but ultimately, we are all accountable in different ways for ensuring a safe working environment.

It was emotionally devastating for me each time I went through this exercise. I didn't like reliving that moment. But it was the most powerful way I could think of to take leadership accountability and create a personal connection to the seriousness of the safety message.

This is not to say that all the responsibility rests on your shoulders. There were many lessons learned from our helicopter incident, each of which required defined corrective action and follow-up. The accountability for the corrective actions rested in various places in our organization, although the tracking of whether corrective actions were accomplished came back to the top.

Extending the value through thoughtful transparency

A thorough identification of root causes puts an organization on a path to taking actions that will actually rectify the problem. This provides a sense of control, and not drifting. It creates confidence both internally and externally that you are steering the ship to calmer water.

Take your commitment to improvement a step further. Make it common practice to use RCA and lessons learned on as many projects as possible. Commit to transparency around your use of RCA and lessons learned. Be willing to share publicly the results of your investigations.

Again, you will likely be advised that it is a mistake in a political environment to take accountability for something that has gone wrong. My experience belied this advice, as long as the release was handled smartly. Make your stakeholders aware that you will frequently use RCA and lessons learned. Use it for projects that on balance go well and learn about what led to making things go right. When a problem project appears, get out in front early by saying publicly there is a problem, as well as describing things that went right. Commit that the investigation will be thorough to find the path forward that reduces the risk of repetition of elements that could have been handled better. This approach lets stakeholders know we are willing to be self-critical. They do not have to dig on their own to identify what is really going on.

The alternative is hoping that nobody will notice. This strategy may work sometimes, but it's Russian roulette. It's possible the problems will not be uncovered by others, but if they are, you will be damned for not disclosing them.

Once your RCA and lessons learned have been shared internally, your odds of keeping the information internal, particularly with electronic distribution of documents, is very low. Given the choices between keeping a close hold and releasing information, come back to core values. Remember the most important question: How does the public interest best get served? Improving the performance of your organization is going to be what's most important to the public.

Your organization will not get better unless you are willing to define what things went wrong, what went right, and then act to learn from them. Making a mistake once is more forgivable than making it repeatedly. The best defense against repeat offenses is to share your learnings across your organization. Ask project leaders to present their RCA findings to others. Catalogue your lessons-learned reports in your library and encourage leaders who are initiating projects to review previous lessons-learned efforts.

The United States commercial nuclear power industry provides an example of improved performance. BPA pays for the full cost and receives all the output from a nuclear power plant, and hence, we developed an understanding of the industry. It is a little-known fact that the commercial nuclear industry in the United States has witnessed a resurgence in safety and reliability in the last three decades. Most people in the industry would argue that this has come about because of a commitment—largely generated through substantial peer pressure—to adopt an unyielding model of applying RCA and lessons learned across the industry, including plants learning from each other.

An RCA in the nuclear industry is rigorous, repeatedly asking why an incident happened until the roots have been reached. The lessons learned are firm commitments to change that have follow-through and follow-up. The nuclear industry has a commitment to model and demand personal accountability.

Continuous improvement is a cornerstone of being a great public steward. A sincere commitment to public service will need to translate

> *"Operational excellence will only be successful if the leader is willing to take on the vulnerability of role-modeling accountability."*

into finding ways to increase the levels of personal accountability into your organization, starting with your own. This can be rewarding when things go right, and painful when they do not. Finding ways to assure lessons are learned and retained in yourself and the organization are critical to improving performance and leaving the world a better place.

Killing "good enough" for government work

Have you ever been in a meeting when a government worker described a product as "good enough," for government work, or something similar. How did you feel when it was said? Did it seem inconsequential, or even humorous? Or did it bother you because it seemed demeaning?

I will admit that earlier in my career I said it more than a few times. I was going along with the crowd and trying to be funny. But it always felt like I was accepting something I actually resented. Ultimately, I took a stance upon becoming the BPA Administrator: I banned the phrase from the workplace (or I at least took the stance that I never wanted to hear it).

When people would say it around me, I would stop the conversation and say something to this effect: *I know that was intended to be funny. And I know that you did not mean it literally. But in a culture where we are attempting to be not just good, but great, it would be a mistake to let that comment pass.*

It grates on me when government work is denigrated even more so when we do it to ourselves. It reflects a culture that assumes our work is less than first-class, and I know it is not. The phrase may be intended as humorous, but it directly undercuts efforts to promote continuous improvement.

The job of leaders is to create the culture we want in our organization. If a sexist or racist statement was made as a joke, we would not stand for it. Treat the degradation of government work—and along with it, government workers—with the same level of disdain. Because in fact the statement reflects a derogatory stereotype. It's a slam, an affront, to your chosen profession. And worse, left not countered, it suggests that sloppy work is OK and accepted. Hence, it risks the threat of becoming self-fulfilling.

We would not want our children to be immersed in a culture that repeatedly tells them they are mediocre, or worse. Why should we allow ourselves to be immersed in very similar circumstances, without objection?

Addressing poor performance

While it is our job as public sector leaders to build employee morale and confidence, we also need to address consistent poor performance. Many organizations underutilize performance appraisal tools, because they are difficult to use.

I wish I could count the number of times I heard that a supervisor had reached a breaking point where they wanted to let an employee go. But when human resources and the general counsel were informed, they did not have adequate documentation. Often, the prior performance ratings were at a level of *meets expectation* or even higher. Documented signs that performance issues needed to be corrected were deficient, or did not exist at all.

It is a public sector leader's role to create a culture that guides and helps supervisors to address poor performance. Poor performers are a cancer in the organization. It's not just that they don't pull their weight, creating more work for others, they are a morale crusher for high performers. The lack of significant financial rewards for high performers can be offset with clear meaning and purpose. But, watching poor performers incur little to no consequences can be soul crushing.

Public sector leaders can take four actions to address poor performers:

First, be clear with your human resource officer and general counsel that their role is to actively encourage and guide supervisors on how to appropriately address performance issues, including developing documentation and personal improvement programs. The goal is to get better performance. Government personnel systems generally create the opportunity for the employee to be notified and improve performance before consequences come into play. Take advantage of these opportunities. Well-written performance plans and thoughtful performance reviews can solve the problem. If not, separation needs to be on the table. HR and GC need to be *partners* with supervisors, not critics who complain that supervisors don't understand performance review processes.

Second, train supervisors in performance management using HR and GC personnel to lead the training. The primary goals of the training are to let supervisors know there is a defined path for addressing performance issues. This takes time, so don't wait until the breaking point to create connections between supervisors and their advisors in HR and GC.

Third, back up supervisors who are making good-faith efforts to address performance challenges. It's difficult for supervisors to give low performance ratings, which can be exacerbated by a perception in government that even if the documentation is complete, no action will be taken. It can be very lonely for a supervisor trying to do the right thing. The employee who gets the low rating/performance improvement plan is not likely to receive it well. Co-workers will often complain about a poor performer to a supervisor, but not confront the poor performer. Dealing with GC and HR can at times be challenging. The performance review processes are elaborate, and the message can easily be that it has not been correctly performed. It's also not easy to get the documentation complete and perform the other elements of your job, especially when covering for a poor performer. Supervisors who take this on deserve your support.

Fourth, make a personal commitment to putting in time to address poor performance within the organization. Build a culture that puts in sincere effort to inspire and resurrect a poor performer, but is also willing to make the separation decision if warranted.

The structure discussed above takes time to put in place, and admittedly, the work to do so is nowhere near as interesting or personally rewarding as addressing policy issues. Yet, addressing poor performance is critically important to building a high-performing organization.

One final thought: If the statutes and regulations will allow, put in place a one-year probationary period for new employees. Making high quality decisions about new hires is challenging. People can look good on paper, or even at interviews, but not turn out to be as advertised. Often, it's better, and procedurally easier, to seek to turn around performance or make the hard decision to separate early in an employee's tenure. I found this to be a rarely used, but very valuable tool.

Conclusion

The helicopter fatality led to a hard lesson that leaders are accountable for everything that happens in their organization. Driving thoughtful accountability through an organization is a critical tool to achieving a high performing not-for-profit organization. It's about influencing the culture in a way that creates wide-ranging positive opportunities to advance continuous learning and operational excellence. It will likely only be successful if the leader is willing to take on the vulnerability of role-modeling accountability.

8

Ethics

It is one of the most beautiful compensations of this life that no man can sincerely help another without helping themselves.

—Ralph Waldo Emerson

One day I was having lunch with a senior state government official. I had invited along a young staffer who I highly valued and wanted to mentor. The state official was seeking a policy outcome that would be beneficial for his state. At the end of the meal, the state official offered to pick up the tab, and I agreed, saying I would get the next one.

Afterward, the staffer questioned whether there would be a "next one," and how I thought about the ethics of that situation. I was at first taken aback. I had refused many free gifts over the years, and felt my commitment to ethical behavior was beyond questioning. Yet, upon reflection, I came to see the reason for the question, and why I needed to change: First, it was uncertain whether there would be a next time. Second, the state official, friendly as he was, did in fact want something from me. Third, and most important, it was my job to set the example.

I had to set the ethics bar high, even beyond what the rules required, if I wanted people in the organization to follow the rules. It was a hard lesson about how I could learn from anyone in the organization, even at times when I thought I was the teacher.

KEY TAKEAWAYS

Ethics violations are the antithesis of public service culture, as they represent public servants acting in self-interest, rather than the public interest.

Ethics challenges undercut all the efforts to increase respect for the work and your people at your agency. It's your responsibility to head off problems in advance by: establishing and complying with a standard that exceeds the current ethics requirements; talking openly with your people about the broad consequences of ethical lapses; and supporting your ethics official.

Unethical behavior is the antithesis of public service culture

Let's say you have been working very hard to build trust in your organization. You are focusing your agency on serving the public interest. You are engaging with stakeholders, creating a culture that treats the public with respect. You are engaged in improving the performance of the agency. It is all very hard work, and you have a right to be very proud.

And then an ethics issue comes along, seriously setting the organization back.

Maybe it's an employee that skirts, or even steps over, the line and gets caught. Such an incident can lead to criminal prosecution, media stories, and a severe mark against your agency's reputation. Imagine how powerfully discouraging and deflating for the whole organization this can be. It also can be internally divisive, since employees may view the severity of the infraction and potential penalties from different lenses. This will shape their view of how management responds.

These kinds of events can be anticipated. As a leader, it is your job to recognize and take preventative measures to reduce the risk of ethics issues arising. The ethics standards in government are high, and they have serious consequences. And for good reason: You are operating as the stewards of assets on behalf of the public. There is an appropriate expectation that public employees will always operate for the benefit of the public good.

The most damaging element of an ethics violation is the dissonant message from the fundamental premise of public service. Ethics issues represent public service employees acting in their own self-interest, rather than in the public interest.

Catching somebody after the violation is necessary, but less than optimal. The goal is to prevent these actions from happening. Below, I outline three tools at your disposal to create a culture of ethical compliance.

Setting the standard

First, your own behavior sets an example. The ethics rules have been steadily getting tougher. It's best just to recognize that what is acceptable today in terms of receiving even token gifts is not likely to be acceptable tomorrow. Earlier in my career it was acceptable to trade lunches. You buy this time and I will buy the next. No longer is that true.

The best advice is to always get a ruling from your ethics official on anything that seems like it might even be questionable. Even then, there may be judgment involved in interpreting the rules. Err on the side of virtue when there is a question. Your reputation is not worth the modest benefit, whatever it may be. Your staff and your stakeholders may rib you about this. But overall, they will respect it, and it will set the tone for your internal culture.

Your people see what you do at work and they repeat the stories. New employees, people from other parts of the organization, or people thinking about applying for jobs within your group will ask what you are like. They will be interested in the type of culture you promote within the group. At some point, the responses will likely get to your perspective on ethics. Your employees will remember if you took the ethics training seriously. They will remember if you turned down a gift, even something small.

Keep in mind that people are frequently watching what you are doing, even when you think they are not. I would be surprised when someone from my organization would stop me at the big-box electronics or grocery store. *Why should I be surprised?* Everyone else goes shopping, too. And while I might be dressed differently than at work, I am not in camouflage.

People are watching, and they are reporting what they are seeing. Not maliciously reporting. It's just idle curiosity. It's an opportunity for watercooler talk. A chance to see what the boss is doing when it appears nobody is watching. We all wonder what people are like when they think they are not being observed. It does not become gist for gossip unless you let it become so.

"Do not underestimate your power as a leader. Sharing your personal views supporting ethical compliance will increase the likelihood of compliance."

Here is a simple rule to follow: Act as if someone is watching you all the time. Frequently, someone is watching you, but you don't know who, and you don't know when. It's easiest to just assume someone is always watching, whether at or away from work.

Setting the tone

What you say does make a difference. Send the signal strongly to your employees about where you stand. Do not just assume that they know.

For example, each agency sponsors ethics training. The timing of the training creates a unique opportunity for you to make a statement about where you stand. Pick something out about the consequences of ethics violations and use the moment of ethics training to speak openly to your group about it. It may make you feel like a killjoy when you are telling your people not to joke around during the ethics training, but it's your responsibility to protect them by making sure they are fully informed. It's also your job to promote the public service nature of the job, and ethics is a key element of preserving the public trust

Beyond protecting your people, you have a responsibility to your organization to make sure ethics is taken seriously. We have all watched organizations lose substantial credibility in the public arena as the result of a few souls who thought they could get away with something that they must have known was wrong. I recall an incident at a public sector organization in which a few employees bought alcohol on company time and enjoyed it in a local park, using government vehicles for transportation. A local television crew caught it all on camera. The ensuing public response led to substantial damage to the organization's credibility.

The problem is that the fallout affects many things that are completely unrelated to the offense. Policy positions that the agency wants to take will be compromised because the agency's political capital has been drawn down. Ethics violations at an agency create a period of time when there is a sense of *who can trust them?*. Moreover, the consequences are far-reaching. There is a huge impact on the morale of the workforce, even for the many people who were not involved in the offense, because they now work for a place whose reputation has been sullied. Their relatives, friends, and neighbors will ask them about what happened, and there is often a hint of whether this is a widespread practice.

As an example of addressing fallout from a potential ethics violation, after an ethics presentation to our employees, I gave a short talk to try to reinforce the seriousness of what had just been presented. I tried to make it personal:

> Maybe it's enough for you to know that your own reputation, and even freedom, are at risk as a result of disregarding the ethics rules. But if that is not enough to convince you, then look around at your colleagues in this room. Prosecuted ethics violations at this agency damage everyone around you. It's as if you stuck a paint brush in a can full of mud, stood on a revolving circle, and spun yourself around as fast as you could. Everyone in this room gets smeared, for something they had nothing to do with, and in fact they may not even know you.

Do not underestimate your power as a leader. Sharing your personal views supporting ethical compliance will increase the likelihood of compliance, particularly when people see you walking the talk.

Viewing ethics officers as key contributors

Finally, recognize what a difficult job your ethics official has—and support them. Ethics officials get to tell employees they can't do things they want to do. And after all, employees would not have brought issues to the ethics officer if they did not want to engage in the activity and press it farther.

I took a variety of issues to our ethics officers, and was often disappointed to find that my own actions were prohibited. Sometimes, I wanted to challenge the conclusion. Yet, the ethics officer would warn me that employees would get the message that the leader doesn't want to comply with the rules that apply to everyone else. Think about not just what you want, but how you will be perceived.

Encourage the development of innovative ethics training programs by your ethics officials. If you run the same training year after year, it gets stale, and so does the message. One effective way to shake things up and make them current is to point to recent stories in the news about ethical lapses. They seem to happen frequently, so you have your pick. Use those as case studies for your ethics training.

Ethics officers play an important role in protecting the reputation of the agency, which ultimately helps make the agency more successful. Help build the strength of the position.

Conclusion

This is one of the shortest, yet most important chapters of this book. Taking proactive measures to reduce the risk of ethics violations in your organization is critical to the success of building a culture of public service that will increase respect and trust. Little things like not exchanging who pays for meals, and big things like speaking about ethics at employee events, are a necessary part of creating a culture of inspired public service.

PART 4

Building Bipartisanship

9

Politics Is Not a Dirty Word

Never doubt that a small group of thoughtful, committed citizens can change the world: indeed it's the only thing that ever has.

—Margaret Mead

I once attended a meeting with a fellow federal executive who led a large regional agency. He shared a series of disparaging comments about elected officials from our region. He viewed them as not having intellectual depth, only looking out for campaign contributions, and willing to vote only along party lines, which made them robotic.

I asked him how he felt his relationships were with the regional Congressional delegation. He said it was, at best, mixed, but there were practically none that he really respected. He felt like he was not succeeding, blaming them for not helping him achieve what needed to be done. Moreover, just participating in the political process of making and administering the law through publicly elected officials was distasteful to him.

This perspective is certainly more the norm than unusual in our culture. We have a long and rich tradition in this country of being disdainful of politics and anyone who chooses to run for political office. In fact, expressing views contrary to this cultural norm can be an invitation to be perceived as naïve.

But building durable, bipartisan solutions is not feasible based on this conventional attitude about politics and politicians. Durable solutions require bipartisan support that can withstand leadership changes through election cycles.

Building bipartisan support requires two elements: respectful engagement with elected officials; and developing a strategy that makes a bipartisan outcome the goal.

It takes finding and approaching elected officials with a commitment to building trust and a sense of working together as a team. A leader must build a reputation around commitment to seeking solutions that understand and balance the needs of competing constituencies.

KEY TAKEAWAYS

The prevalent deeply cynical cultural bias against politics and politicians must be overcome to be successful at crafting durable solutions. It is important to recognize and acknowledge the institutional role politicians play for representative democracy to succeed.

Make a paradigm shift away from our cultural norms. Give the benefit of the doubt that elected officials have similar public service motivations as your own. Consistently build trust through collaboration on the shared objective of serving the public interest.

An important paradigm shift is to think of elected officials as fellow public servants also seeking to serve the public interest. Don't buy into politics being unseemly. Think of it as the expression of democracy. Consider the impact of the terms of reference you use, such as *elected official* versus *politician*.

Understand how an elected official's institutional role creates limitations on subject-matter mastery.

Build trust with elected officials based on:
- Respecting the strengths of their institutional role
- Sharing knowledge freely
- Avoiding being in sales mode
- Recognizing constituent interests
- Getting your decision processes right
- Providing objective analyses
- Staying situationally aware
- Understanding the political process
- Sublimating your personal preferences
- Using thoughtful decision releases
- Celebrating success

Grassroots engagement and support will be respected by elected officials, which increases the potential for gaining broad support. Start with a strategy based on understanding the views of key legislative and executive branch officials. Build solutions engage affected parties formally and informally. Set up interactive discussions with elected officials about how their parties' views are evolving during the policy development process.

Establishing trust creates the opportunity to build on success and reap a trust dividend.

When the challenges seem overwhelming, envision the unsatisfying alternative to producing bipartisan support.

Respectful Engagement: Overcoming Cultural Bias

We live in a culture that is disparaging toward politics and politicians. Even the use of these words is frequently taken as derogatory: *Oh, it's all about politics*," or *Oh, he's just a politician*. There is a strong hint of mendacity, of unsavory character, that focuses on self-interest and an unwillingness to work for the common good.

Certainly, there are politicians guilty of operating only from a perspective of self-interest. Moreover, the pressures of campaigns and elections can cause even those of the highest integrity to lose focus on occasion, attributing it to the importance of not losing to a poorly qualified opponent.

Yet, it is important to separate the anecdotal from the rule. Do not fall prey to allowing preconceived cultural biases define your interactions in the political process.

Have you ever walked into a discussion where you had the feeling that you were pigeon-holed because of who you were perceived to be? Maybe it was the general lack of regard in our culture for public servants, and you knew they were not likely to give credit to ideas that originated from within your agency. Or maybe it was a case of regional differences, where accents are enough to leave the impression that you are starting from a deficit position.

If this is a situation you have had to confront, there is probably a fair amount of baggage you are carrying. It becomes a challenge you expect to have to deal with, especially when meeting someone new. Now think for a moment about what it must be like to be an elected official. What it must be like to regularly face distrust, just for choosing to provide public service through an elected office. Public officials are subject to a form of discrimination. They expect bias against them because it happens so frequently; sometimes, they see it even when it is not intended, or are slow to believe that there's still someone out there who may not be a practicing member of the cultural faith that all politics and politicians are self-serving. On the other hand, they can also be deeply appreciative of those who respect the importance of the role they are fulfilling.

There is substantial risk to democracy from having a public that actively opposes its government. We contribute to that risk by being dismissive of or disdainful toward politics and politicians, and not recognizing the value they must provide for democracy to be successful.

During my career, I have had the opportunity to be in more than a thousand meetings with members of Congress, Governors, or state legislators. In most cases, these were private meetings meant to discuss pending issues within my agency that had consequences for their districts. I also participated in the more public arena, testifying before Congress, regulatory agencies, or state legislatures. Being an exhibit at Congressional Town Hall meetings was also part of the job.

My impression from these discussions is that, with rare exception, elected officials were very interested in hearing about the facts and discussing the principles being used to help make decisions. It was not unusual to have my meetings run longer than scheduled, waving away the scheduler who entered the room to provide the *it's time to move on* stare, responding that there are not enough meetings that are really about policy. They loved it and made time for it.

The vast majority of publicly elected officials are people who got into the field because they wanted to make a positive and meaningful difference in the world. Anyone who walks into meetings with Congressional members, or other publicly elected officials, thinking otherwise is setting themselves up for failure.

For anyone who chooses to serve the public interest, it is critical to keep in mind the intent behind our democratic form of government. It is the people through their elected representatives who govern. Step back from personalities and consider elected officials in their institutional role; allow them to make the contributions needed for democracy to flourish.

When done well, the executive and legislative branches can work symbiotically. When done especially well, bipartisan solutions to difficult problems can emerge and be adopted. What is critical to understand is that as a leader, you have the opportunity to make a contribution to creating a better world through defining solutions to seemingly intractable problems. But it will take establishing a paradigm shift in your own thinking, one that often runs counter to cultural norms, and hence, difficult to sustain both intellectually and emotionally. You may be ridiculed as naïve. Yet, starting by giving trust is more likely to materialize in success than leading with cynicism.

You can be the catalyst for positive change, or just another cog in the cultural machine that threatens our democracy. It's your choice.

The Paradigm Shift: Politicians as Fellow Public Servants

The phrase, *it's all about politics*, has over time become increasingly lacking in sophistication for me. If it means using deceit to gain public office, of course that deserves to be condemned. But if it means politicians seeking to get elected by responding to the views of the people they serve, that should be celebrated. That is the essence of representative democracy. Frequently, I see these two concepts becoming conflated.

It takes fortitude to willingly choose to participate in defining the public interest through seeking public office. It is more worthy of our praise than the condemnation it elicits in our culture. It is almost certain that anyone standing for public office will receive more intense scrutiny of both their values and their personal life than any other profession.

Now this is not to say that every politician is deserving of respect. Of course, there can be dirty politics, just like there can be corrupt business practices. But we don't automatically think of business as a pejorative term. No professions are free from scandalous behavior. Politics is populated by human beings, some of whom will be flawed, and most of whom are worthy of our respect.

The question is where one should place the benefit of the doubt. I assume they walk into the public arena with the same sense of commitment to public service that I have. They have their roles as defined by law, representing a specific set of constituents. But most members that I interacted with were also interested in the implications of a policy proposal at a larger scale outside their district—for the region or the country. They were interested in more than partisan implications.

It is age-old advice that to get trust, one must give trust.

Now I need to be careful not to lead readers astray. Starting from a position of trust does not mean trust no matter the circumstances. Certainly, a few elected officials did not respond to my approach in a trustworthy way. I had to change my approach to those that were untrustworthy, or risk repeatedly being taken advantage of and losing credibility with other elected officials. But I had so many positive experiences by leading with a willingness to trust that it more than offset my negative experiences.

The willingness to start with an expectation of working together to solve problems is key to building a collaborative environment dedicated to serving the public interest. Check your own thought process and language. If you choose to be disrespectful toward politicians outside of their offices, it is quite possible that your feelings will come through when you walk into that office. It is very difficult to be successful in the public arena while simultaneously being disdainful of the political process or politicians. Most likely your staff has picked up on your cues. The culture inside your organization will also tend to diminish the value of input from elected officials.

The paradigm shift necessary for success in the public arena starts with believing that politics is not a dirty word. Politics are the expression of democracy. Politics are the attempt to convince voters that a certain set of ideas represents the best expression of how to serve the public interest. Participating in the political process, particularly as it relates to the setting of public policy, is a necessary and even enjoyable part of working in the public sector.

Even the terms we use are influential. Consider the difference in reaction when the term *politician* is used versus *elected official*. I tried to avoid using the term *politician* in the workplace. It simply induced a negative reaction that caused people to overlook opportunities for finding common ground.

If you choose to be a public servant seeking to make a positive difference, then likely you will need to spend time in the world of elected officials. This is ultimately where the determination of where the public interest lies in a democracy.

Understand the limitations and the opportunities

There are limitations on the role politicians can play, particularly in an increasingly complex world. Recognize these and adapt to them. The expectations for elected officials range far beyond what any human being can possibly accomplish. The typical member of Congress in a single day will move from a discussion about an international hot spot, to tax policy, to implications of the federal deficit, to the need for a new infrastructure investment in their district. It is unreasonable to think that members can become intimately familiar with all these subjects. It's just as unreasonable to expect members to understand an issue as well as someone who is a specialist in the field. We should not belittle elected officials for finding it difficult to identify workable compromises given the complexity of issues.

This dispersion of focus in the legislative branch creates opportunity for people with subject-matter expertise. There is a depth of knowledge within any government agency regarding policy options and implications of complex issues. Subject-matter mastery should be a core competency for government agencies. This depth of knowledge can be used in many cases to help define options and engage conversations that can lead to bipartisan solutions.

Building trust and teamwork

Building durable bipartisan solutions begins by building trust with elected officials who ultimately will define whether the solution actually is bipartisan. I offer a few suggestions below for how to build that necessary trust.

Creating team through respecting the institutional role

An important opportunity to build trust begins with assuming that you are dealing with a fellow public servant serving a role as defined in the Constitution. Elected officials are more than just another member of the public. They are the elected representative of the people. You may agree or not with their perspective, but they took the incredible risk of choosing to stand for election. To allow the public to judge whether their positions and values are worthy of support. That the government is run by elected representatives of the people is the critical element of democracy.

When viewed from this perspective, elected officials tend to take on a very different aura. No politician comes away unscathed from public criticism. Moreover, every politician is a human being and has flaws like the rest of us. If you choose to focus on the idiosyncratic *peccadillos* of individual politicians, you will find there will always be much to dine upon.

Approach each meeting as an important opportunity to engage and gain understanding from a person who has been granted the role of elected representative of a group of citizens. Someone who has willingly taken on this role in order to do their best to create a better world. Start from the perspective that they deserve respect for the role they are serving. Be aware of how they have been described in popular media, but do not make that the basis for your interaction.

Elected officials have the best, most current, information about how the public we are all seeking to serve defines what best serves their interest. When we combine the depth of subject-matter expertise in the executive branch with depth of knowledge about the public's perspective, we create a recipe for producing good public policy. I tried to think of all elected officials as members of my team, and me part of theirs, in the search for how best to serve the public.

An interesting value evolves from seeking to engage as colleagues. When approached as people who are providing essential input to the decision, elected officials can become your scouts. Elected officials are great leading indicators of how the public interest may be shifting. Legislators, due to their frequent contact with constituents and their fellow elected officials, have tremendous understanding of how the public interest is evolving. They have a huge advantage in terms of understanding the mood of the public over those of us operating within an agency.

When starting from this perspective, it becomes easier to think about the development of policy as a team effort in which you are effectively teammates.

Public comment processes provide excellent avenues for the public to express its feelings on a specific issue, but that knowledge is enhanced by that of an official who must stand for election on a regular basis. There were times when I was telling elected officials about what their constituents were thinking, but frequently, they were providing insights to me.

How you approach these engagements will likely influence—if not control—your likelihood of success. Recognize elected officials are carrying out an incredibly important and necessary function for our democracy to work. Don't focus on the individual, but more on the institutional roles you are both engaging. Seeing the engagement on a higher plane, recognizing the institutional roles in the democratic process, establishes a foundation for respectful engagement.

Sharing knowledge freely

Elected officials are usually very interested in getting the facts in an objective way. Nobody wants to take a position that turns out to be substantially ill-informed. As civil servants with the task of understanding issues deeply, we have value to offer elected officials. I noticed that elected officials often suspect that they are only getting a part of the story, and there is a tendency to press to *get the other side.*

Share your knowledge in an objective way. A great trust buster is leaving the sense that only one side of a controversial story is being told. A great trust builder is laying out the array of policy advantages and disadvantages, and then testing options with elected officials, who are also serving the public interest.

Avoid selling

As a leader, you will undoubtedly have an opinion on the best course of action on important issues. You might feel a tendency to share only the supportive information for the option you favor with elected officials, so they agree with your current view.. In my career, I recognized there was always a risk that my meeting with an elected official could be used as a basis for a public statement; and, I always wanted them to support me. Resist the temptation. Instead, provide an array of perspectives. It's a better long-term strategy toward building a relationship based on teamwork. This kind of relationship builds stronger long-term policy, and programs. When you open up the range of perspectives, elected officials will often reciprocate, introducing views you might have not yet heard.

Nobody more a person who stands for public office comprehends the importance and relevance of elections. They understand that an executive branch official needs to reflect the will of the head of the executive branch. What they are looking for is whether you are remaining open to finding solutions that represent the perspectives of as many citizens as possible.

Recognize constituent interests

Keep in mind that an elected official's designated role in democracy is to represent their constituents. Elected officials tend to have a hair trigger on whether their constituent views are being heard. Missing or misrepresenting an important view from within their constituency can lead the elected official to negative perceptions about whether the process is being conducted in a fair way.

To build trust, present a balanced view of what various parties are saying and present a focused understanding of the views of the elected official's constituents. Thinking of yourself as a fellow public servant, it's important to be an objective purveyor of facts.

If one leaves the impression that the views of a significant interest group are being ignored, expect trouble. Elected representatives will believe it to be their duty to express those views, and likely in a vigorous way. If, however, they believe efforts have been made to understand the perspectives of their constituents, seeking common ground wherever possible, it will influence the direction of their public comments.

Get process right and provide objective analyses

In the political arena, process can be easier to argue than substance, simply because process (and process fouls) can often be more easily understood by elected officials than the substance. Thus, the way public service leaders represent the issues leaves a distinct impression on elected officials regarding whether the process is being conducted in a trustworthy manner.

Another way to generate credibility with elected officials is by initiating public processes that assure all the options are on the table, even if just in a generic fashion. Then assess the ramifications, again in a fair and objective way. This means trying to make sure all proposals for how to address an issue are included, even ones that you might find odious.

Providing objective analysis is a tool that can be used by anyone seeking to participate and influence the political process. At Chelan, we were part of a group of utilities that chose to support analysis by independent consultants who assessed least-cost approaches to goals for carbon-emission reduction. The analysis assumed reducing carbon emissions is important, as is addressing affordability and reliability of electricity. The work created a strong framework that was well received in the Washington state legislature. It also built credibility to support further investigative analysis on pressing public policy issues. The key was not defining an acceptable answer in advance, but to work through the analysis to objectively learn, and then share.

"I tried to think of all elected officials as members of my team, and me part of theirs, in the search for how best to serve the public interest."

Seeking advice

Another opportunity to build a sense of team can be found in seeking the advice of elected officials. When discussing a controversial issue, describe the principles you will use to try to make the decision. See if there is an important principle you have missed. Talk about how people will be impacted. It helps connect to the official, opening the door to insights they may be able to offer.

It also opens the door for the elected official to see how the views of their constituents are juxtaposed to other public-interest concerns. This can often change what would otherwise be the public position of the elected official. They can better see the trade-offs involved in the decision.

Be open to what you can learn. Elected officials have to give a great deal of thought to how things will be perceived. This is not always obvious to those of us who do not spend all our time in a perpetually publicly visible world. Hence, elected officials are often able to provide great insights about how policy or program proposals will land in the public arena.

A willingness to bring elected officials inside the decision-making tent as a colleague, even if only privately, is a cathartic event. You may get useful advice on either policy or presentation that you would not have expected. It happened frequently for me. If you are truly open to advice, you will need to be a patient listener/student, as well as teacher. Be prepared for opportunities to learn.

Moreover, whenever one can find a way to use some of the advice offered, it creates greater opportunity for buy-in when the decision is announced.

As a young staffer, I sat in on a meeting between my agency leader and Senator Slade Gorton, from Washington state. My boss explained how an issue that was generating significant controversy would impact various constituencies: There was a small group of communities that would be heavily impacted by the proposed policy, but the majority of people would see a small benefit. Essentially, the message was that the majority should prevail. Senator Gorton taught us an important lesson that day, however: Voters may have views on lots of issues, but they vote on only a few. Something that would drastically disrupt the lives of a minority may still outweigh the views of the majority—if the issue is not that important to the majority. Polling alone cannot be the basis for decision-making in democracy. This may seem elementary to seasoned political professionals, but to us it was an important insight. It influenced how the agency managed the issue.

Stay situationally aware

There will be times when the sense of collegiality you are seeking to engage will feel tread upon. There was one member of Congress I dealt with who would on occasion issue press releases right after our meetings, describing how he had harangued me on an issue of concern to local constituents. That did not feel good, because it cast me in the light of needing to be chewed out to understand something I thought I understood pretty well. It also raised concerns from stakeholders on the other side of the issue, since I might have been unduly influenced by the input I had now publicly received.

The path I chose in these circumstances, unless there was something factually inaccurate in the press statement, was to shelve my pride and recognize the elected official was merely attempting to let his constituents know he was fighting for them. I'd also be proactive about letting key stakeholders and other elected officials know through off-line communications my interpretation of our meetings, as well as the aftermath.

Knowing that his press statements were bound to happen from time to time, I would try in our meetings to describe the actions that would benefit his constituents that were actually within my grasp to deliver. In this way, hopefully he would make his public statements about actions that were within the realm of the possible, rather than urging a policy that had no chance of being implemented.

This is a critical step because it gives elected officials a chance to look good by advocating for a policy that actually could be implemented. The alternative—having an elected official call for a particular outcome that cannot be delivered—is likely to result in their public opposition to the decision that does get made. Seldom do elected officials back down from a public statement. Begin early to lay the groundwork for policies that can generate bipartisan support. Inform elected officials with the options that can benefit their constituents *and* are within the realm of the possible, and explain why.

Engage early

This brings us back to a point worth repeating. Recall the concept of *the concrete is drying* in the public arena, from Chapter 6. To create a sense of team, it is critical to engage early and quickly to assure that public figures see the full horizon of issues that must be addressed, particularly before they begin making public pronouncements.

Display respect by learning the political process

Ever had someone approach you with their good idea that is not based on reality, but they still expect you to implement it? Maybe they don't understand statutory constraints, who has the authority to make the decision, or the roles of various actors in decision-making. It can feel like a waste of your time.

Similarly, in our democracy, officials have defined institutional roles that need to be respected. Approaching key players in the political process with a lack of understanding of their role in policy-making processes can border on being disrespectful. While it's not obvious in the media, public policy is usually made with various agencies and elected officials playing a role. Don't just walk in asking for help. Know what role each official has a responsibility to play.

Sublimating your personal preferences

Once input is solicited from elected officials, there is an obligation to use it in a meaningful way to develop solutions that reflect as much as possible the perspectives you have heard. If one believes publicly elected officials have the pulse of the public interest, then they provide critical input to a decision that serves the public interest.

For example, the Pacific Northwest represents some of the most liberal and conservative Congressional districts anywhere in the country, ranging from very Democratic areas west of the Cascade Mountains stretching north and south and including Seattle and Portland, to one of the most Republican states in the Union, Idaho. One can approach that range of views and assume there will be no common ground. Or one can listen very attentively and find pieces of issues here and there that if adopted would help to make a decision more palatable to all concerned.

There are big themes that generate consensus, which sometimes partisans can find surprising. The economy and jobs are important to everyone, for instance. Interestingly, environmental protection is another common theme. Partisans can attempt to divide by claiming their opponents don't care about one or the other. But nearly universally, I found in private meetings that members of both parties, even at the fringes of their party, are interested in creating legacy that finds ways to unite the goals of economic and environmental health in common purpose.

There can be moral hazard in taking this approach of serving the public interest as the public seeks to define it. There will likely be times when your own values may be in conflict with those of the public. There were times for me that the will of the people went at least a few degrees different from what would have been my own preferences. In those situations, I worked to make sure the public had the same information I did. But, if there was a consensus that produced bipartisan support different from my own predilections, than I believed it was my responsibility to sublimate my values to those of the public.

This may have been one of the hardest parts of public service for me. There were times when I felt the public was making a bad choice. But my conclusion was that if I could not convince significant stakeholders of the course of action I wanted to pursue, then I had an obligation to serve the public interest as the public saw fit, or else seek a new job.

Conclusion

If the reason you are in public service is to make a meaningful and positive impact, then building durable solutions should be a goal. Durable solutions are most likely with a bipartisan approach where policies are not up for review each election cycle. My colleague referenced in the beginning of this chapter sadly ended his career in frustration. Great success is achieved through accomplishing what was previously believed to be unlikely, or even impossible.

In the next chapter, we consider how bipartisan solutions are built from outside the legislative process.

10

Bipartisan Solutions from the Bottom Up

It is better to light one small candle than to curse the darkness.

—Confucius

I always wondered why somebody didn't do something about that. Then I realized I was somebody.

—Lily Tomlin

In the public sector, we operate in an environment in which much of the conventional political wisdom is based on the politics of the day. Yet, political circumstances evolve unexpectedly, making what was previously impossible suddenly achievable. But it's only possible if what seemed like pointless effort was pursued until the right moment came along.

For many years as the manager of the Washington, DC office, I advised BPA Administrators that there was no chance to increase the ability of the agency to borrow money from the US Treasury for needed infrastructure investments—despite strong indicators that the investments had a very high likelihood of being repaid *with interest*. During that time, there was simply too much focus on federal deficit reduction. Then, after the west coast energy crisis of 2001 I felt constrained as the BPA Administrator to make the infrastructure investments the situation screamed out for. The absence of borrowing authority for capital projects was a key reason the agency was not doing more. So, I had no choice but to make the case for increased borrowing authority, even if it appeared futile.

Lo and behold, the 2008 economic crisis led to the American Recovery and Reinvestment Act. In December 2008, I met with a former energy expert from the Clinton Administration who was advising the incoming Obama Administration. What we at BPA had wanted for many years was what the incoming administration was looking for. Our team was able to quickly provide relevant constituent and bipartisan Congressional support. By spring, what six months earlier had seemed impossible became law.

Two lessons from this experience. Conventional political wisdom is likely right today, but may be wrong tomorrow. Plowing the field for a good idea during periods of low probability of success is necessary to be ready for the moments of opportunity.

KEY TAKEAWAYS

Building bipartisan solutions starts with defining strategy that believes bipartisan solutions are possible.

Create value in public comment and meetings, rather than check-the-box exercises. Use informal dialogue to build belief that bipartisan solutions are possible.

Keep elected officials in the loop. Take time to formulate thoughtful decision-release plans. Go out of your way to celebrate success.

The previous chapter speaks to the importance of relationships with elected officials and their staff. Strong relationships with key policy-makers provide the capability to get to bipartisan solutions. The really hard work, though, and the place where an executive branch official can have the greatest influence, is in the field with constituents.

While elected officials are a great *leading* indicator of where the public interest lies, they are also an excellent *lagging* indicator of how well you and your agency are doing in treating their constituents with respect that leads to widely supported bipartisan solutions. If bipartisan actions are not forthcoming, start by taking a look in the mirror.

Get to know key constituencies affected by policies within your realm. Earn their respect by getting to know their interests and their views on issues.

Start with strategy

If you want your result to reflect bipartisan support, you need to have a strategy. Any good strategy starts with where you are and where you want to be. What does bipartisan support for your conclusion look like? Who in particular would be supporting it? Where do you stand now with those key people and the influentials surrounding them?

Go back to the concept of the political influence map in Chapter 5. Who are the key Democrats and Republicans in the executive and legislative branches who have the combination of the greatest influence and interest on the issue in play? Who are the key influentials that will in turn influence these key actors?

There is a certain amount of judgment that goes into making these determinations. Sometimes, it might be senior people within the administration. Or it may be a committee or subcommittee chairman. Other times, the issue may take on a distinctly local flavor, leading to a junior member of the legislative branch or a staffer being the key player. The key is knowing early on who is likely to have the greatest impact on defining the position that other leaders will rely upon.

From there, build your strategy for engaging around the people whose support will be needed to get to a bipartisan outcome. Who are the key influential parties that will advise key decision-makers? Who within your sphere of key constituents overlaps with key decision-makers? This will help define where to focus your energy.

The most difficult part of this assignment may be getting people to believe that you are seeking a bipartisan solution, especially in this day and age. To achieve this, you will need to take some radically counter-cultural perspectives. It takes wearing your commitment to public service and developing bipartisan solutions on your sleeve.

The value of public comment and meetings

There can be tremendous value in public comment, both written and oral public comment. Public officials miss out on valuable opportunities for finding common ground when they choose to read only summaries, or even worse, choose not to participate in public comment sessions.

Most commenters choosing to engage in the substance of an issue do not want to appear foolish, and hence, spend considerable time thinking through the arguments they will make. Frequently, in the course of developing these arguments, they will find data that had previously not been on the table, flaws in the logic of the proposing agency, likely consequences that might not have been previously visible, or even flaws in their own logic, causing them to say it differently than before. Sometimes, even better, they find an opportunity for compromise. For reasons that are not clear to me, often these important points can be missed in a summary of comments. I chose as much as possible to read the unvarnished comments, or at least as many as possible. This turns out to be not as difficult as one might think, because many comments can be skimmed as duplicative.

Having a good understanding of the written public comment creates the opportunity to maximize value from oral comments.

I found it very valuable, although time consuming, to attend some public meetings. This contributed four elements that written comments alone could not provide. First, sometimes the comment was just too dense (or I was too dense) to get the point. An oral rendition, combined with the opportunity to ask some questions. could help to clarify an otherwise obtuse point.

Second, often the written comments just did not capture the level of emotion associated with a particular issue. Intensity of emotion matters in the political arena and it's important to understand where the intensity exists and why. The personal angst a citizen may feel is hard to convey in writing. Some of my most poignant moments came in public comments from ordinary citizens who were able to capture the magnitude of the impact of the decision on their lives, their family, or their neighbors.

For example, I still vividly recall a rather small meeting regarding the impact of a large rate increase we had put in place. One official from the school district explained in simple terms the financial cost: the trade-off the school district had to make in terms of number of teachers they could employ and the ripple effect on students. In another instance, a woman explained that her family lived on a farm that had been in the family for five generations. She explained the cost impact to them relative to their other costs and revenues, leaving it clear the continuation of the family farm was at risk. The tremor in her voice would never have come through in written comments.

In many ways, this was the most rewarding part of the work, because it brought home the meaning and importance of the decision. It brought home the public service aspect of what we do. It made me want to work harder to try to find better solutions. There is a sense of gravity that causes a decision maker to dig deeper, to seek solutions that can generate more widespread support.

Third, sometimes there is information that would not otherwise be available because of local knowledge. It may be the history of the place, the geography, or the culture. Each community is unique, and local knowledge that can improve a decision is hard for an agency to gain without discussions with local folks.

Fourth, meeting in a public forum provides a chance to engage people on the difficult trade-offs you are confronted with as a decision-maker. Each proponent of a proposal will have good reasons for why their proposal should be adopted. But they may not voluntarily address the proposals from other parties who they oppose. This creates an opportunity to engage in conversation about various public interest values. Do proponents of proposals that create jobs see merit in concerns from the environmental community, and vice versa?

When confronted with a decision maker who is willing to ask questions and contrast the positive attributes of the positions of various parties, there is often an opportunity to find more common ground. It also gives you the opportunity to try to take the commenter beyond speaking only to their self-interest. It helps them see what it is like to live in your shoes. It pushes constituents to think about the larger question of what best serves the public interest.

Meaningful engagement with commenters on the question of what best serves the public interest in a public forum can be emotionally difficult. At least for me there was a tendency to want to agree, or at least nod, as comments were being made, particularly if there was a lot of emotion. Put another way, there is the pressure that offense will be taken if anything other than agreement is offered.

Yet, being willing to engage a commenter on their view of other perspectives can yield valuable ground for compromise. I would tend to want to ask if the commenter had felt or heard any common ground with others whose positions appeared to be in opposition. If given the chance to comment on the difficult trade-offs facing the decision-maker, at least some members of the public will engage and seek to find ways to meet multiple public interest objectives.

"If you can establish yourself as a person who seeks to find solutions that are nonpartisan and successfully implement them, your ability to resolve future issues is greatly enhanced."

Informal Dialogue

Public agency leaders can easily be trapped in their bureaucratic towers, feeling that it may be risky or beneath them to engage in informal dialogue where ideas are just being tested. Agency counsels tend to be conservative about informal outreach. If there are adopted *ex parte* rules, they must be abided. I found there were frequent opportunities to push the edge of a lawyer's comfort zone. The benefits of informal dialogue were high, since better understanding was created on both sides.

Personal outreach efforts to leaders of key constituencies who believe they will be impacted can result in finding new alternatives or mitigation that might help mollify the discontented. Sometimes people feel they can't say in public what they are willing to say in private. This is particularly true if they have heard the other side either in person, or directly from you. I used to try to initiate conversations such as these with a comment on the order of, "It seems like the other side made a good point when they said…."

Do not give up easily, even with people who you believe are your enemies. People who engage in the public arena do not like to be ineffective. Provide them avenues to express means for a policy to be improved if it can't be defined exactly as they wish. And, even if you cannot find some common ground, it will build a bridge for engagement on future issues.

The theme here is to actively pursue people's support, or at least neutrality. Broad support will often lead to bipartisan support. Even diligent efforts to develop broad support may engender bipartisan support.

This all leads to a simple conclusion about how to best pursue bipartisanship: *Listen attentively wherever you go.* This requires tremendous patience, the reservoir of which is usually at its greatest in the early years of a new job. Listen for common ground. Be the most knowledgeable person about the subject because you have listened attentively.

Beware of thinking that you know what someone is going to say before they say it. That is a clear sign that you have outlived your usefulness, because human beings are constantly thinking and evolving. A mentor taught me this: What seems like a repetition of yesterday's statement may be true for 90 percent of what is said. But the speaker may have generated a new thought that slightly alters the perspective and takes what was previously an issue at loggerhead, turning it into a moment of opportunity.

The fervent pursuer of bipartisanship is an attentive listener and prober. It can be a thrilling journey much like any other kind of hunt: a scavenger hunt, or a hunt for wild animals. Imagine for a moment the feeling of all senses being engaged in the hunt. The most successful hunters are the ones who are most resourceful, most engaged, most determined, and ultimately can best identify the relevant clues for success. In this case, the quarry is successful bipartisan resolution of an issue.

Strive to address the biggest, most difficult issues to resolve. You may need to start small to get to the bigger ones, but keep your eye on the issues that are the most controversial. Why? It's a simple calculus. The most controversial issues are the ones most important to your stakeholders, and thus, most important to serving the public interest.

Finally, commit to seeking opportunities for collaboration among affected parties to help solve the problem. Government decision making can frequently take on an air of quasi-judicial process that is managed by attorneys. Seek to break out of this wherever possible.

Find ways to bring competing interests together and urge them to seek collaborative solutions. This can be as simple as sharing alternative views in small-group meetings to generate feedback on whether there is any common ground. Or asking someone their view on whether there are any thoughts that have merit in opposing comments. This can go as far as creating forums for dialogue between groups with opposing views.

Leaders have the power to convene and to establish the agenda. Use it to promote collaboration that hopefully can lead to cooperation.

Keep elected officials informed and engaged

Take time to establish a two-way flow of information with elected officials that pulls them in to decision making, offers them a significant role, and gives you better insight as to what options best create opportunities for durable solutions. Assuming you have developed a respectful relationship with elected officials, there will be opportunities throughout the process to share information about how affected parties are reacting to various proposals.

Thoughtful Decision Releases

The final step, one that is often inadvertently overlooked—undermining months or even years of great effort—is the roll-out strategy. Getting a decision announced properly turns out to take much more planning than most would assume. Moreover, there is no second chance on a roll-out. Mistakes are difficult to repair, because initial opinions are hard to change. Roll-out mistakes also undermine confidence in your agency's ability to manage policy process.

Rule number one is that key parties who may comment publicly on your policies know when you are going to release decisions—at a minimum. It's best if they can be provided some sense of the direction on how the decisions are going, and why. While this is obvious, it can be hard to implement.

The policy development process can be grueling, especially for controversial issues. Usually, all the available time has been taken up just making the decisions. And the deadline is pending. There is a need to get the documents out the door. Yet, this is the moment when as a leader you must create a pause. Create focus and consider: who are the critical parties that will be impacted by the decision, who are the elected officials that are most likely to react, and who have the greatest influence (see the influence map in Chapter 6)?

Advance notice with those parties helps to shape their reaction to the policy through the common courtesy of not surprising them. Many of the political pros will advise you in this moment to share little, because the opportunity of advance notice will be turned on you with preemptive releases from your opponents. While I did not ignore this advice, I would try to push closer to the edge on the side of telling officials at least when something was coming and hinting at, if not outright telling the outcomes. Building trust is the key, and one must be willing to take some risks in terms of trusting others if one wants to be trusted.

A critical associated piece is the old rule of a lot can get done if one is willing to give others the credit. Generously give credit to any and all that have participated in the process, especially elected officials. Ask elected officials and key stakeholders in advance if they would be willing to publicly support the policy, and include them in your announcement if they are.

If public support is too much to ask of certain public figures, test to see whether you can gain agreement on the next steps which, hopefully, becomes the focus of their response rather than opposition to the policy. Many times, there are opportunities to work together on next steps.

Celebrating success

A person who became a good friend over the years taught me an important lesson about how to build on success. Ron Suppah is former chairman of the Warm Springs Tribe in central Oregon. He was a key partner in developing agreements regarding salmon restoration that moved many tribes from opposing the government's position to supporting it.

He urged from the beginning of our discussions that we see the potential in celebrating success. He used the potential for a public celebration as motivation for the government and tribal teams that were negotiating the agreements. Everyone could see that this would be an historic agreement, helping satisfy everyone's desires to do meaningful work. He also strongly urged us to hold an annual celebration of the agreements that were signed. This was designed to help bolster the foundation of trust between our organizations we were seeking to accomplish, going beyond just the terms of the agreement.

Ron wanted to change the culture between our organizations from one of antagonism to one of cooperation. Sitting down annually in a celebration event, reviewing the accomplishments, reminding ourselves of how far we had come in terms of building a positive relationship. While planning and organizing the event was time-consuming, Ron was right that it made our teams feel proud of accomplishing a difficult, but rewarding change in our relationship.

It also reminded both the government and tribal personnel that we did not want to go back to the way things had been. The celebration reinforced our desire to resolve any currently outstanding issues in a manner that built an even stronger legacy of partnership.

Such celebrations are just as important in the political world. When bipartisan solutions can be identified and implemented, they and the elected officials who helped make it happen need to be celebrated. Celebrations reinforce not just the particular accomplishment, but the underlying relationships and trust, making future negotiations more likely to be successful.

Celebrating success can take many shapes. There is the traditional ribbon-cutting event where all the contributors to success gather. There are the press releases that acknowledge all the various contributing actors. One of the most effective approaches was taking advantage of the opportunities afforded when speaking with or giving speeches to constituents impacted by a successful resolution to a controversial issue. In that situation, there is high value in going out of the way to call attention to the group of key players that caused a bipartisan solution to emerge, particularly the people who represented the specific constituency being addressed.

The Trust Dividend

If you can produce success on the high visibility issue, there will be a greater willingness on the part of elected officials and constituents to work with you on issues going forward, big and small. It doesn't mean that you can reduce your level of commitment to resolving issues. It does mean it may take less effort because a perception grows as to how you will approach issues, including more of a willingness to seek compromise. There is greater confidence the result is not likely to be one-sided.

The trust dividend is real, and my agency has been a beneficiary. After we at BPA had worked through some very difficult high visibility regional issues with Native American tribes, a series of local issues followed that impacted reservations or ceded territories. Our foundation of trust allowed us to manage through these local issues with greater speed and success than would have been possible otherwise. These issues, such as transmission line sitings, were very important to us, and them.

It's true that trust can be mistreated, and an attitude develops like this: *So you think you are going to get whatever you want because we are friends now.* From the beginning of the relationship, you must bring a willingness to believe that the other side will come in good faith to understand the concerns and seek to address them. The trust dividend grows with each joint accomplishment, and provides more fertile ground for succeeding at finding mutually satisfactory solutions in the future.

The same is true in the partisan world. If you can establish yourself as a person who seeks to find solutions that are nonpartisan and successfully implement them, your ability to resolve future issues is greatly enhanced. The willingness of political figures to share what they really need increases, accelerating your ability to define workable solutions. In many cases, your reputation will precede you, particularly in discussions with, new members of Congress, for example.

Getting on the right side of being given the benefit of the doubt is necessary if you intend to be more than a one-issue pony. Success begets success, because the trust dividend gets larger with each issue that gets resolved.

This entire discussion of engaging with publicly elected officials comes down to a simple rule: human relations matter in politics. Treat people fairly and with respect, and your odds of getting a better outcome go up. Moreover, your odds of getting to a more collaborative relationship on the inevitable next issue are also greatly increased.

Don't believe bipartisanship is dead

Reading the headlines, it would be natural to conclude that bipartisanship is a thing of the past. It would seem that anyone seeking to work in a bipartisan fashion is a cute, but ineffective anachronism. A dodo bird attempting to survive in the political world.

My experience belies this perception. In the Introduction, I described that my selection and retention in a high-visibility job in the executive branch was supported on a bipartisan basis across more than a decade. There are strategies and tactics that can be employed to increase the likelihood of bipartisanship, even in today's rough-and-tumble political environment. Certainly, there are some big-picture issues on which the Democrats and Republicans appear to be in perpetual disagreement. An effective leader has to be aware of them in order to successfully enter the political arena. But, there are many other issues that government addresses, and your approach can help define whether the issue will be addressed in a bipartisan way.

In fact, there are many recent pieces of legislation enacted that required bipartisan support. The media focuses on controversy, so we mostly hear about the areas of disagreement. At the end of the 2020 legislative session, for example, Congress passed legislation that was primarily described in the media as being about providing relief due to impacts of COVID. But the bill is comprised of over five thousand pages, including appropriations bills, and at least seventeen authorizing bills addressing water resources, energy, foster youth and families, health insurance, aircraft certification, and more. This took bipartisan support, since at the time the House was controlled by Democrats, and the Senate by Republicans. There was a lot of partisan dispute that led up to its passage, but it passed in the House 359-53, and in the Senate 92-8.

Conclusion

Getting legislation enacted is very difficult. What's really hard is successful enactment of bipartisan legislation. However, if the goal is to create positive and meaningful improvements, then the higher bar is where to set the goal. Going back to the beginning of this chapter, the projects that were eventually built with increased borrowing authority are still providing benefits today, and will for decades to come. Success on this level takes being willing to ignore the cacophony of voices saying bipartisanship is dead. It takes being ready for the moment when unexpected opportunity presents itself. It takes a commitment to believing good public policy can still be achieved despite conventional wisdom.

PART 5

Developing Your Leadership Style

11

Communication

Great leaders are almost always great simplifiers who can cut through argument, debate and doubt to offer a solution everyone can understand.

—Colin Powell

In the public arena, opinions are constantly being formed. Being early, accurate, and good at communicating is critical to achieving high-quality decisions in the public sector. An extraordinary mentor of mine whom I worked with for several years emphasized the *early* part of communication. Our conversations were often lengthy and frequently heated. And as I recounted in Chapter 6 on decision making, I could always count on him repeating one phrase: *The concrete is drying*. What he meant is that opinions are more malleable in the early stages when there is ongoing discovery. The concrete is wet in this stage and more easily shaped. But once opinions are formed, they become like dry concrete. The level of effort necessary to chip and remake opinions goes up exponentially.

KEY TAKEAWAYS

Recognize oral and written communication are key to building trust that you are acting as a good steward of the public's assets.

Consider four rules for communicating:
- Center your communication around your public service ethic and what you are trying to accomplish-—using your mission, vision, value and strategic plan as foundational.

- Understand the substantive material of the issue at hand with the depth to be able to communicate concisely and accurately.
- Seek to engage in dialogue.
- Choose to overcommunicate.

Start with empathy rather than authority. Be open to ignoring what feels like personal criticism to search for legitimate public policy concerns.

Communication is the cornerstone to building trust

Communication is even more critical to the success of a leader in the public sector than in other sectors because of the responsibilities that come with serving the public interest. Communication, written and oral, provides the vehicle to explain purpose, describe values, set expectations, and seek input for decisions being made on behalf of citizens. Effective communication is also the key to establishing the trust necessary for government and democracy to work.

If mission, vision, values, and strategic plan are in place, communication becomes much easier because nearly all communications refer to these source documents as their foundation. This creates consistency in message, and that in turn helps to build trust.

We know being perceived as trustworthy is critical to the success of a public sector leader. Communications convey a window into the values the leader embraces. There are many decisions a leader makes that are out of public view. The public must make an assessment as to whether they believe a public sector leader has the right motives to serve their interests, even when nobody is looking. This is true whether the leader is in a high-visibility position or rarely in the spotlight. Great communication can lead to a belief that a leader's heart is in the right place and deserves trust.

Choosing public service means acting as steward on behalf of the public. A good steward will do their utmost to accomplish the vision of the community they are serving. This happens best if there is a deep level of understanding of all the community's desires matched with the options that are available. To achieve that level of success, you need great two-way communication.

Four simple communication rules

There are four simple rules I offer with respect to a leader's communication responsibilities that build a public service culture:

- Center your communication around what is most critical to serving the public interest based on your mission, vision, values, and strategic plan. Remind stakeholders of your public service motives that are driving the events that might be creating stress for them.
- Know enough about the subject matter to be able to speak concisely and accurately.
- Engage in meaningful dialogue. Be proactive about seeking engagement. Be willing to listen and seek ideas that will improve the solution.
- Communicate early and frequently. Aggressive communication provides the opportunity to assure key decisions that will impact the public are understood, leading to more pragmatic and valuable comments. It's nearly impossible to overcommunicate, especially in a period when the stakeholder is experiencing increased stress.

Centering communication around serving the public interest

By centering both your speaking and written communication around the motive of serving the public interest, you engage stakeholders at a level above their own self-interest. When this happens, they better understand the main question always at stake: *What does the most to improve the quality of life for everyone affected?*

It is easy to get distracted by the technical complexity of whatever issue is being addressed. It is important to understand this complexity and ultimately to communicate it. But the starting point needs to be the largest picture of what is at stake for the public interest. Think back to your mission and vision statements. What elements are impacted by the issues you are discussing? Now convey that connection.

Consider how you would explain the issue and what is at stake to your friends, neighbors, or relatives. Doing so tends to pull us in the direction of thinking about larger messages and connecting to values that are important to the public. And getting away from acronyms.

With enough practice, the goal is to get comfortable at explaining issues to a larger audience in a compelling manner. There is nothing more compelling than speaking concisely and accurately.

Speaking concisely and accurately

Successful communication requires deep understanding of what you are communicating. Merely being able to repeat the talking points is not good enough. If that's all you can do, then there is little opportunity to engage in problem-solving dialogue if the receiver has concerns with the message.

To be a successful public policy maker requires being able to translate technical complexity into policy *concisely and accurately*. It is critical to be able to do both. Many people can do one or the other. Speaking concisely, but not accurately will win you applause in the short term and a deficit of trust in the long term. Speaking accurately, but not concisely will leave you with an audience that is unwilling to hear you because it is taking too long and is difficult to understand.

To be able to speak concisely and accurately, you have to put in the time to understand the issue from a variety of perspectives. When conducting a course-setting meeting, do not leave the room until confident you can describe the issue concisely and accurately to your upper management, and to constituents. Use the five decision factors from Chapter 6 to assure you have comprehensively examined the issue. Think about whether you can convey the key issues at stake that are important to the public interest . When a decision is made, be prepared to describe how it best serves the public interest. Speaking concisely and accurately benefits the public when you explain your recommendation or decision, and within your organization, and staff will see how serving the public interest guides your decision making.

There has been a tendency in the last decade to encourage managers to delegate and get out of the way. There is value to that school of thought. Managers should not be doing the technical work. That said, managers need to be conversant in the work that is being done, as well as the challenges faced. Managers also need to know how to measure the quality of work being performed. Asking probing questions allows one to get a better grasp on the difficulties in getting the work accomplished. Those difficulties come in two broad categories: The first is a situation related to process, where the work is getting done, but it is being accomplished inefficiently. The second gets to the fundamental value trade-offs that represent the essence of public policy making; these must be understood at the executive level.

"As stewards of the public's assets, it's our responsibility to be great at communicating opportunities for the public to understand the issues and provide meaningful input."

Sometimes value trade-offs may not be recognized at the working level. But a good leader needs to have the ability to comprehend the issues that are going to generate public controversy. It takes keeping antenna up with respect to what the big picture issues of the day are for your agency. You need to make the connections to the broader scope of issues that others working for you may miss. You need to think across the functions of your organization to assure recommendations and decisions are integrated, to avoid siloed approaches.

An excellent leader can understand the work that is underway in their group and be able to predict the likely potential public controversies that could potentially arise. A superior leader has enough depth of understanding of the issues that they can describe them both concisely and accurately. This is very difficult to do. It requires being able to quickly go between 30,000 feet and the ground, and back again.

Engaging in dialogue

With all the time spent understanding an issue well enough to describe it both concisely and accurately, it can be hard to pause and listen to other points of view. Yet, defining the public interest can only be accomplished through understanding where the public's interest actually rests.

When working with profit as the primary motivator, understanding what is happening with prices in relevant markets is critical to success. Similarly, when serving the public interest is the primary concern, it is critical to understand how the public defines its interest.

And, just like markets are constantly moving, the public interest is dynamic and constantly shifting. The importance the public places on issues such as the economy, national defense, or environmental protection will take higher or lower significance at various points in time.

As a leader in the public sector, you must understand how the public is defining its interest relative to the decisions you need to make. Communicating issues and getting feedback in a constant iterative loop is as critical to your job performance as staying current on commodity markets is to a trader.

There are two things needed to be successful at engaging in dialogue:

First, you must engage. This may be hard because it means taking risk and exposing yourself to criticism. Take the plunge and reach out to both your potential allies and foes. Both will appreciate your willingness to engage. Do it informally, over meals, or formally (e.g., regularly scheduled meetings with interest groups).

Second, you have to be willing to listen and really hear what people are saying. Look for ways to incorporate their thoughts, despite concerns that their ideas might generate a negative response to the solution when presented . It may be that most of the input you get from a particular group or interest is not helpful, but often there can be a nugget of new thought that creates the opportunity to work collaboratively and improve the proposed solution.

Communicating early and often

Too often, people assume that basic efforts to communicate, such as issuing press releases, are adequate. Often it appears the public is not really listening, anyway. Most of the public we serve seems too busy to hear our messages much of the time. But the challenges associated with finding out what people think don't mean opinions are not being formed.

We should not translate an inattentive public into believing there is no need for people to be sought out to engage in the decisions of their government. We should recognize that *the concrete is drying* even when we think nobody is watching. Communicating early to describe key issues, what's at stake, and the realistic alternatives leads to more informed engagement.

We must compensate for what appears to be indifference by seeking opportunities to regularly share information about key policy issues. Sometimes, stakeholders don't understand what is at stake until late in the game. Then they become frustrated, frequently attacking the process for not being adequately inclusive. Choosing to communicate early and often reduces the likelihood of decisions being revisited because the public discovers late in the process the impact on their lives. It also helps decision makers understand the public's views as they are evolving.

Seeking to communicate frequently creates an additional benefit: it can help to encourage calm. A lack of information creates opportunities for speculation, most of which can be so far from the truth that it is barely recognizable. A constant flow of information, even when the solution is unclear, allows people to focus on the real issues and what is actually at stake.

Here's an example of the power of frequent communication:

One Monday morning, I got on a United Airlines flight headed for Washington, DC. I had meetings scheduled about ninety minutes after our planned arrival. As we were preparing to push away, the pilot informed us that a light had come on indicating the flaps were not working. A few minutes later, he came back on and said the problem was fixed. We pushed away, but as they started the engines, the pilot announced that the light was back on. So we went back to the gate. And sat there for an hour.

During that time, however, every ten minutes the pilot came on the PA to report on the progress to fix the problem. He placed a great deal of emphasis on recognizing the impact the delay may be having on the passengers, and the sense of urgency the airline felt to get it fixed. We got a report whether there was any news or not. With every report, he reminded us of the importance the airline placed on safety.

Normally, during a delay like this, I'm fuming. I start thinking of all the reasons why we might be sitting there—and most of them have to do with the incompetence of the airline. But this time, I was pretty calm. Just having the flow of information with words that came across as sincere and committed to providing high quality service to passengers reduced my anxiety. It helped that I had not hit the point, at least not yet, at which I needed to postpone my scheduled meetings.

Finally, the problem was fixed and we took off. During the trip, the pilot gave us reports on how they were working to make sure everyone made their connections. For example, they had received special clearance to fly at the altitude that maximized the speed of the plane. The pilot also appealed to passengers not at risk of missing connecting flights to allow those who were to exit first.

My reaction to all this was, despite the delay, a sense of increased loyalty to the airline because I had been treated in a respectful way. Now, if the mechanical failures occurred on a regular basis, I'm sure my patience would run thin. Good customer service requires being excellent at the fundamentals of the service being provided. But when the exception occurs, your approach to communication can make a world of difference between a good and a poor experience.

My experience on the plane is indicative of how many people react to similar policy-making situations. When policies are developed in secret and dropped with little warning or engagement, the result is little understanding of either why or what is happening. The negative reaction can get magnified. The issue gets translated into a matter of lack of respect. And in our form of government, with many checks and balances, a party believing they are not being treated fairly is going to find an avenue to express their displeasure.

There is another important element in my flight to DC: The pilot chose to engage us, less from a position of authority, and more from a position of empathy. It's a good example of how we should handle ourselves as government employees engaging with the public.

Starting with empathy rather than authority

You work for the government. You may not sometimes realize it, but you have authority—always. You represent everyone who works for the government all the way up to your chief executive. If you work for the federal government, that means all the way up to the President, and for the state, up to the Governor, etc.

There are many times our policies place stress on people. Sometimes we are downstream from the source of the problem, but we are the face the public gets to deal with. Be prepared to take responsibility to communicate vigorously. Seek to enter these interactions from a position of empathy and kindness. Limit use of the authority role to only what is necessary.

Sometimes in interactions with the public, the comments from frustrated citizens can become personal, or they can feel personal due to the accountability we take for both process and substance. I tried to view these as moments where someone was trying to get my personal attention. The antagonists are looking for a commitment to address their concern. I try, not always successfully, to put myself in the shoes of others before reacting. What is their fundamental concern—beyond process—to the substance? Do they have a point, even if weakly articulated? It can be hard to inject objectivity into your assessment of the criticism, especially when your team is also feeling defensive. Making good public policy, though, requires separating the wheat from the chaff in public comment—even when the wheat may include criticism.

In public meetings, learn how to read the emotional level of the room, especially when questions come from upset citizens. Sense any changes in the people around you. And be aware of what your own feelings mean. It may be the feeling of unease, anger, or frustration. Frequently, there is a desire to respond quickly, to want to counter an accusation and not let it go unanswered. In a public meeting setting, the heightened emotions might drive you to respond in ways that are really more directed toward winning over the audience than to pull the other person into dialogue.

We all know this feeling, and it is a typical human response. It can happen in deliberative process as well as public meetings. It takes a conscious assertion of self-control to provide a response that will change the course of the conversation. The meeting leader needs to take charge and pull the emotion out of the discussion.

Easy to say. Hard to do. In these moments when emotions run high, there is substantial risk that the meeting or process will go south, and be difficult to recover. The conflict will dominate people's recollection of what happened at the meeting, no matter what you accomplish.

As I was leaving the BPA, a fellow employee recalled a phrase that I used that seemed to help in these tense situations: "That took courage to say…."

This is frequently true for the speaker. Odds are their heart is pounding as the conflict escalates. When there is substantial emotion involved, it is likely that the person had to work up their courage to make the statement. They are confronted by their government—which is large, omnipresent, and frequently overwhelming. Creating a personal connection changes the dynamic and opens a path to problem solving. Recognizing the courage of the person offering critique can change the course of an internal review of comments away from a defensive reaction to looking for where there may be substantive value.

Just to be clear, this approach cannot be used repeatedly in the same meeting, and will definitely not be successful with what I would call *the professional rabble rouser* who is seeking to speak to the crowd and positional bargain. But with people who are really seeking to speak to you, and raising legitimate concerns, there is an opportunity to create a connection.

The matrix that applies to public speaking (see Chapter 12) applies here as well. It is just as critical that you know your audience, whether speaking one-on-one, in small groups, or to a large crowd. That allows you to frame the discussion in terms that are important and meaningful to the receivers.

Conclusion

As stewards of the public's assets, it's our responsibility to be great at communicating opportunities for the public to understand the issues and provide meaningful input. Don't let the concrete dry. Be proactive, accurate, and concise to assure the right information is available to allow effective discussions leading to high quality decisions.

In the next chapter, it's time to get to an even more personal level of communication: giving speeches.

12

Giving Speeches

People don't care how much you know until they know how
much you care.

—Teddy Roosevelt

Midway through my career, I realized that I wanted to be an organizational leader. That led me to recognize that I would have to be a public speaker. So I began to seek out public speaking opportunities. I think it's safe to say that at first I was terrible. Pathetic even. Frequent public speakers know that people who approach you after giving a talk will invariably compliment your speech. But even that didn't happen for me in my initial forays.

But something changed. In my first few months leading BPA, I was being asked to speak in many different venues about the west coast energy crisis. The impacts of the energy crisis were overwhelming. There was much the public needed to know, and it was constantly evolving. I didn't have time to try to be a speechwriter, seeking the perfect turn of phrase which I could only remember by reading the speech.

I found myself in Seattle where I was putting my notes together in the hour before I was to speak to a group. I started with our motivations as a public sector, not-for-profit organization. I focused on things I uniquely knew that the public needed to know. Knowing the audience, I tried to connect to their interests. I did my best to articulate that we were extraordinarily concerned about how the continuing energy crisis would affect the public. I quit trying to emulate speakers I admired and spoke as conversationally as possible. For me, that means speaking quickly because I had a lot to tell them.

Afterward, an acquaintance who had spent years following BPA said it was the best speech he had heard a BPA Administrator give. I needed that feedback to realize I had my own style. It may not lead me to be an Abraham Lincoln. But I could be good if I focused on being myself. Ultimately, I learned from that experience that there is a formula for giving speeches that worked for me to capture the hearts and minds of the audience.

KEY TAKEAWAYS

Public speaking is hard for most of us. But, developing the skill is a necessary part of leading especially in the public sector. Done right, it helps build trust necessary for democracy.

Choose to use public speaking as a means to promote the public service ethic. Connect the subject matter to your mission, vision, and values. Use it externally to explain why and how decisions will be made. Use it internally to drive a culture built around public service.

Use speeches as an opportunity to connect with your audience, but also to explain the perspectives of others as a means to build bridges across difficult issues.

When formulating speeches, consider a matrix built around your mind and heart, as well as your audience's mind and heart. Be sincere when talking about your public service ethic.

Recognize there are differences between speaking to internal and external audiences with a particular focus on describing serving the public interest as driving decisions when speaking to internal audiences.

The best way to get better at public speaking is to find learning opportunities to practice.

Public speaking is integral to success

Public speaking brings out a sense of dread in most of us. Yet, it is a challenge we must overcome in order to be leaders. If you are going to be a leader, you will speak in front of groups. Speeches are a particularly crucial tool for articulating and driving a vision around the public service ethic. Important internal and external audiences are observing the power of connecting and persuasion that you bring to speaking appearances.

I like to view a speech as an unparalleled opportunity to build trust, since giving a speech provides a window into the character of the speaker. People come to know who you are through your descriptions of what and how you think, and they form lasting impressions about who you are and what you stand for.

Recognize that when you are asked to speak, it is usually because of your position. People want to know about your thinking regarding the issues you have been charged to address. Yet, sometimes speakers get confused about what is important to convey. A few of the key errors I have made, or I've seen others make:

- Speaking about subjects that may be on the mind of the audience, but for which the speaker has no more expertise than audience members (*Why is he talking about that?*).
- Not speaking about principles that are key considerations to the issue at hand. (*Where is she going?*).
- Speaking without connecting to circumstances that are familiar to the audience (*What is he talking about?*).
- Not including references to principles that are important to the audience (*She doesn't seem to know what is important to us!*).
- Not speaking concisely (*OMG, how long is this going to go on?*)
- Not speaking accurately (*He either doesn't understand, or else intentionally misled us.*).

Professional speech writers know all this and are good at using words to connect people intellectually and emotionally. Most of us don't have professional speechwriters, or even if we do, are not good at reading a speech someone else wrote. Other than for the gifted speech giver, it's especially difficult to be sincere with a speech someone else crafted. For the rest of us, we need to plot our own approach.

Here is a simple matrix that can be used to test whether your speech will be well-received. Within the context of your subject matter, but not necessarily in this order, talk about: what you uniquely know and think; what you value; the relevance for your audience; and what they value. All of this is within the context of speaking concisely and accurately.

Your Mind

Speak about what you know, what you have expertise in, what you think about. You have access to information not available to your audience or else you likely would not have been invited to speak. Don't speak about things anyone could know who has access to popular media. Share your specialized knowledge. You also know something about how decisions are being made and how the audience can be involved. Talk about what you uniquely know and think about subjects that are relevant to them. Share that knowledge in as concise and accurate a way as possible. Avoid the acronyms unless you are confident they are in common usage throughout your audience.

The easy part of a speech is telling an audience what you know that agrees with their perspective. This helps build a reservoir of goodwill. But speeches are also a great opportunity to explain the perspective of others, to help build bridges. This is true whether speaking to an audience of issue advocates, or speaking to staff about a management perspective. A good speech both connects to and teaches an audience with the goal of helping to build common ground across stakeholder groups.

Your Heart

When speaking about difficult issues, speak from your heart as well as your mind. Speak to what you believe in. Include a connection to your organization's mission or vision statement. Share the key values you believe are relevant to the decision process. Let people know what is important to you.

For me, every speech was an opportunity to communicate the importance I place on public service. I would share how I consider serving the public interest as part of my decision-making process. For example, I might relate that I didn't always select the option that I thought was best if there was a strong, broad, and informed stakeholder view on an alternative legitimate public policy choice.

I would try to speak to at least one of our values. Stewardship and trustworthiness are meaningful to many different audiences. They can create emotional connections to an audience, even for members who may not be familiar with the subject at hand. I would explain how the decision-making process would be connected to our agency core values.

Usually, an audience wants to know something about what you are like as a person. It's an important opportunity to connect your public service values to current situations. Developing a collaborative process that results in broad support would almost always be on my list.

This can also be a good place to describe your agency in terms of the dreams of its founders. Historical references are helpful to connect your audience to a larger vision. How is the public interest enhanced by the existence of your agency, and how do the founder's dreams relate to the issues of today?

A focus on speaking from the heart is an opportunity to display a commitment to inspired public service. When the audience connects emotionally, it sets another brick necessary to rebuild the foundation of democracy created through increasing trust in government leaders.

Your Audience's Mind

Speak to your audience in terms of what your actions will mean for them, not what it means for your agency. What is the relevance to their life, their job? For example, acknowledge and display understanding of the impacts (e.g., environmental, rates, jobs, etc.) on particular communities that are represented in the audience. Too many leaders make the mistake of speaking about why the subject is important to their agency. Possibly interesting, but not audience-connecting. Use specifics relevant to the audience. When talking about jobs, define the number and quality within the community the audience represents. If talking about the environment, display understanding of the interconnected impacts across various ecosystems with a focus on those most important to the audience.

Recall the discussion about being able to explain to your friends, neighbors, and relatives what is at stake and how it connects to your agency vision. Make eye contact with your audience members. See if you are connecting about matters that are important to them. In nearly every large audience, someone is going to be nodding their head in the front row. How are you doing with the people in the middle? Are they staying engaged?

Your Audience's Heart

Go beyond the intellectual and speak to your audience's values. Know your audience, particularly what they believe and feel. What is it that motivates them? Before you get on stage, be familiar with the key values that are important to them and relate to those values in ways that are sincere and meaningful to you.

"Public speaking is one of the best opportunities to build the trust necessary for restoring confidence in government and democracy."

Are you informing them, or seeking to get them to take action? Usually it is the latter. If you want action, you need people to connect both intellectually and emotionally, even if it is just expressing support for the activities you are leading.

Use personal examples of things you have seen or done that have brought their values into practical meaning for you (e.g., visits to specific communities and people). Possibly, that means embracing their values. It could mean acknowledging their values as their reality, if you do not feel connected. Or possibly, it means challenging their values because there is a larger public interest at stake; if this is the case, also highlight other key values that you and the audience share.

Speaking about creating legacy will usually strike the heart of an audience. That's why so many speeches refer to impacts on children and grandchildren. For many people whom I spoke with about BPA issues, for example, preserving the economic and environmental value of the hydropower system for the people who live in the Pacific Northwest was motivating to them.. This long-term perspective was a shared value between my audience and me.

Do not have a one-size-fits-all speech. Speak to the topics your audience is interested in. Use terms your audience would use. Before you start your speech, try to ask someone in the audience what has been on the agenda that had intrigued or energized the crowd. Seek to connect with that issue someplace during your talk.

The matrix—your mind, your heart, your audience's mind, and your audience's heart—can be used to guide the development of your speech. As the use of this model became more natural for me, I would use it as a checklist after I had prepared a talk to make sure I was not missing a key point of connection. Whether you use it to prepare or to assess a speech, the matrix helps assure you have not become self-absorbed in the minutiae of your own thoughts, but are treating the speech as if it is part of an ongoing dialogue. But it only works if the values you espouse show a sincere commitment to public service. You have to believe to succeed.

A Learning Opportunity

One of the most crucial speeches that I have made happened when I was the BPA Administrator, a story I shared in the Introduction of this book. At the time, BPA was proposing to reduce electric power supply during the west coast energy crisis that would have effectively shut an aluminum facility. Continuing to serve the plant meant buying power at an incredibly high cost that would be passed on to all regional electricity consumers. We were even committed to paying the aluminum companies an amount that would assure the workers would receive their wages and benefits as if they were still working. The net cost reduction to all our other ratepayers justified the action.

My learning opportunity arose when the roughly four hundred aluminum workers and family members arrived to picket outside our office. They wore t-shirts emblazoned with *Wright is Wrong* and chanted my name outside our building, urging me to visit them. I did not want to give a prepared speech because I felt the lack of sincerity would be poorly received. But I was worried about whether I would find the right words in the moment. It was clear, though, that they had traveled hundreds of miles to speak with me, not anyone else, and I needed to respect that. I also felt that we were sympathetic to their plight, willing to work with them, and wanted them to know that. So, I chose to speak to the group. I still remember vividly being led through the densely packed crowd to get to an hastily erected stage, feeling like there was no training that could prepare me for that moment.

My goal was to explain both what I knew and what I felt, and to connect with them on their knowledge and emotion. I started by reminding the audience that BPA is a public service organization, without a profit motive, and that we were seeking to find the best answer for everyone involved in a difficult situation. I explained the challenges confronting us, the impacts to others in the region if we continued to provide power to the aluminum producers, and how they fit into the larger picture of serving the public interest. I also stressed how we were willing to work with them to mitigate the economic harm they would suffer.

One thing I felt confident about was that I could explain, concisely and accurately, the circumstances, our choices, and our concern for them. BPA's position was that shutting the plant was the best choice from a societal perspective, and that the economic gain to other ratepayers could be shared with the workers to leave them no worse off than if the plant were operating.

I also wanted to connect with them in terms of the value their jobs created to their communities and their families. I had visited the mostly rural communities where aluminum was made. I wanted them to know that I understood and was taking into account the critical nature the family-wage jobs provided that helped make their communities good places to live.

It ended up being a rewarding experience because many said the circumstances had not been explained to them in that way before. There was opportunity for dialogue with individuals after I spoke. Many of them gathered tightly around me, once again raising the hair on the back of the necks of our security people. I heard from one very articulate woman the impact of lost taxes to the fabric of the community. That led to a decision to add a payment to cover the lost taxes. It was fair compensation for the benefits the rest of the region would gain from closing the plants. Moreover, it began a relationship that allowed us to work collaboratively for more than a decade, although there were many more in a series of t-shirts to follow: (e.g., *Wright is Really Wrong*, *Wright is Still Wrong*, until the last one, twelve years later, *Wright Got it Right*).

Sharing knowledge and heart in a public setting can be both emotionally gut-wrenching and tremendously rewarding. Overall, strong, lasting relationships are built that lead to better public policy solutions.

Another lesson from this experience was the importance of not only what makes sense from a societal perspective, but also to seek to distribute the societal benefit with individuals who end up being hurt. The goal should be to try to create a societal net benefit, with no losers. This can best be accomplished through dialogue with the most affected parties.

Internal vs. External Speeches

There are many similarities between internal and external speeches, but one very important difference. With internal speeches, you are seeking to define and establish culture.

When speaking to your employees, it's important to be incessant when addressing how serving the public interest drives decision-making. Speaking repeatedly about the core values that have been adopted emphasizes their relevance. It creates a culture that believes leadership is committed to making public service the driving principle for what gets done and what gets rewarded.

Sincerity is necessary to be successful at establishing culture. Don't use other people's words, unless they particularly resonate with you. Use your own terms to describe your commitment to public service and how it guides you. Don't be afraid to speak about what drove you to public service.

Repeatedly make the connection between public service and the need for continuous improvement. Continuous improvement can be threatening to people. It represents change, and change is always hard. Connecting continuous improvement to public service provides the higher calling for why it is both necessary and appropriate. At BPA, I would try to connect our actions to the fact that millions of people in the Pacific Northwest effectively buy our electricity. When we can find cost savings, we are putting disposable income back into people's pockets, and potentially saving jobs that would otherwise be lost.

How to get better at public speaking

The only honest assessment I can make of my first forays into public speaking is that they were terrible. By the end of my career, I was much better than when I started. Beyond developing the heart and mind formula, practice was integral to my improvement.

It was hard for me to get up and do more speeches after suffering the failures I experienced early on. But I knew I wanted to lead, and that I could not lead without getting better at public speaking. Classes did not work for me. The only thing that worked was trying and trying again to get comfortable speaking in front of groups. I constantly asked for feedback from audience members, as well. Possibly the best advice I got was to not try to be like anyone else, but speak at what was my natural pace (which is fairly fast) about things that I thought about a lot because I cared about the issue.

I used avenues outside of work, as well. Any chance I could get, such as being involved with community service organizations, I would find a way to speak to groups. It was painful for many of my audiences, but it put me in a position of being ready to lead when my time came. If there was a video recording of the speech, I asked for it. Seeing yourself speak is a powerful way to learn.

Finally, I try to never give a speech without practicing it once by myself. Yes, talking to yourself in your office or your bedroom can seem awkward and uncomfortable. But it is far better than hearing your speech for the first time when you are giving it for real. There is something about hearing the words that makes it different than when it's in writing, whether notes or a full script.

We have great tools now because any mobile device has recording capability. You can see and hear your practice. Storing your practice sessions can also be rewarding when you can look back over time to see how you have improved.

Conclusion

Everyone needs to find their own style for successful public speaking. But the four elements of speaking about what you know (mind) what you feel (heart) and connecting to your audience's mind and heart will help to build the culture of public service and respect that creates trust. Public speaking is one of the best opportunities to build the trust necessary for restoring confidence in government and democracy.

13

Getting Ready to Begin, and to End

There is no greater challenge and no greater honor than to be in public service.

—Condoleezza Rice

In the summer of 2001, I was riding high, mostly. The incredibly high prices in wholesale electricity markets had abated to normal levels. Aggressive initiatives to increase supply and reduce demand had reduced our proposed rate increase from the 250-percent range to 45 percent, with a reasonable expectation that those numbers could be decreased through time and focused attention. Still way too high, but aggressive management had made a positive difference. Much to my surprise, I was asked by the new leadership at the Department of Energy to stay on as the permanent leader of BPA, with the unanimous endorsement of the eight United States senators from the Pacific Northwest.

But in one important way, I was not succeeding, if not failing. I was good at making policy calls and generating external support. My leadership team at BPA, though, was uncomfortable with my leadership style. In tentative and somewhat varnished comments, they encouraged me to evolve and grow.

Given the external applause I was getting, it was hard for me to clearly hear the efforts at constructive criticism. With hindsight, I can see that I made decisions haphazardly and autocratically, with the justification that we were in a crisis and action was needed. The biggest problem, though, was that I had given a lot of thought to the decisions a BPA CEO needs to make, but not nearly enough about how to manage a decision-making process. I did not have a philosophy about how to manage through structured processes that allow the rest of the team to meaningfully engage.

163

There are two important days in your leadership role that don't get enough attention: the day you begin, and the day you finish. Thinking ahead allows you to be ready for both.

KEY TAKEAWAYS

Prepare yourself for leadership by observing leaders and decision-making processes. Take the time to consider how you would act if you were in charge.

Observe how structure, from mission definition on down, can successfully guide decisions.

Watch and learn how high-quality decisions are made through engagement of individuals representing various disciplines, evolving toward consensus.

Imagine being responsible for decisions important to your organization. What values would be important to you if you had the accountability?

Prepare yourself for departing the job when it is best for the organization.

Be ready for criticism after leaving a position, as there probably are areas where improvements can be made. Everyone has strengths and weaknesses. Weaknesses lead to blind spots that are likely to become more obvious once you leave.

Be prepared that your successor may find less need for your advice than you may feel is warranted.

My Experience

I had not prepared adequately to lead an organization when I first assumed command. My excuse was that I had only a couple of weeks notice, but upon reflection, I had years when I could have been preparing; instead, I was focusing on whether the decisions in meetings reflected my views. Consequently, early on, I made a lot of mistakes because I had not given enough thought to how to lead and motivate. I had people offer to help, but I didn't take full advantage because I didn't know what I didn't understand.

Having learned from my experience at becoming a leader, I knew to consult experienced leaders about how to know when to leave. I was better prepared when my time came. Still, there were some things I had to experience to fully learn.

Prepare yourself for leadership

No matter where you are in your career, there is almost always someone operating at a higher level in the organizational chart than you. When you are participating in a decision-making process in which you are not the decision-maker, but are close to the decision process, go beyond just thinking about what input is needed from you. Seriously think about what you would do if you were in charge.

How would you manage the process? What information is at high enough quality to make a decision, vs being sent back to staff to improve? What key element of a quality decision might be absent from the field, and needs to be brought into view? How does the decision fit with the mission, vision, values, and the strategic plan of the organization?

These kind of questions are best asked when sitting in a decision meeting, especially when earlier in one's career you are a back bencher. Sure, you have an important role and you are ready to play your role when needed. But there may be large parts of the meeting where your role is not necessary. Don't waste your time just sitting there.

Imagine you are leading the meeting. As you look around the room, are the right elements of the organization present to make the decision, or does someone need to be summoned? Is the leader managing the meeting to get the necessary information on the table? What decision would you make? Could you summarize the decision before the decision-maker does? Are all follow-up actions and accountabilities defined? Does the decision reflect the vision and core values of the agency? Could you explain your decision concisely and accurately?

Finding opportunity

If you are a go-getter working in public service, there are frequent opportunities to participate in and contribute to decision making early in your career. It happened to me when in only my second year, my agency began to contemplate terminating construction on two nuclear plants.

I have to say I was enthralled by the chance just to attend the meetings during which the decisions—which had many elements, and stretched over an extended period—were made. Everyone knew these were momentous decisions that would reverberate on front pages across the Pacific Northwest. I watched seasoned veterans of the agency grow incredibly tense at the magnitude of what was at stake, go into great depth about the complexities of the issues, and then resurface to summarize what was important and what was not. There was tremendous focus, frustration, occasional humor, but always an understanding of our responsibilities.

I was so enthralled and caught up in the decision itself that I mostly missed the opportunity to think about and learn from the process that was being utilized. But here I was, starting a career that would last more than forty years, during which I would repeatedly be involved in critical decision processes, many of which were well-run, but some not.

Unfortunately, what I learned from these nuclear-plant meetings was pretty much by osmosis, as opposed to critical analysis and reflection. I was obsessed with the decision itself, which I had decided early on I thought I knew the answer to, based on only the information I had gathered. I dismissed consideration of the other elements of the decision. I did not pay adequate attention to the decision process, which is critical to assuring a sound decision gets made. I did not closely observe how the leader was allowing various points of view to be aired, allowing a group consensus to emerge.

Don't make my mistake. The opportunity to learn from observation is a skill that can be used throughout a career. I still watch meetings, whether as a participant or outside the process, to see how local, state, or national leaders are managing the decision process and defining the values that should be used to make the decision. Imagine yourself in the role of the decision-maker whenever possible.

Making the right decision

While considering the decision process was not my strength, I was preparing myself early on by focusing on what constituted a decision that best served the public interest. I'll say again, decisions in the public sector can be much more difficult to make because there is not a single profit/loss bottom line. The definition of what best serves the public interest is more vague and a matter of interpretation. Multiple good

> *"If you think you have heard it all, you are wrong, and it is time to move to another place where everything seems new to you."*

causes are at stake. Use every opportunity to practice key decision-meeting by asking how you would define the public interest if you were the final decision maker. What decision would you make?

One of the hardest things for new leaders is clarifying their values to the organization, and externally. When confronted with choosing between multiple laudable objectives, what rises to the top for you? In a tough choice between protecting the environment or jobs, what would you choose? How about how much public money to spend on a public safety action?

Being around decisions is not enough to make this clear. Only being responsible for decisions really makes it clear. But you can do the next best thing by assuming the role of decision-maker, even if only in your mind.

The Beginning

Have a philosophy about how you want decisions to be made. As outlined in this book, you can start with mission, vision, and values, which lead to strategic and performance plans. Or you may have a different approach. What's important, regardless, is that the folks working with you can see how decisions are made: Where their input is needed and welcomed. How decisions flow from an organized set of principles about how to best serve the public interest.

In the beginning of a new job in leadership, there are a lot of people watching. Your staff wants to know what your expectations are, not just for policy, but for how work will be performed and decisions made. Be ready for that moment with views about the culture and values that you want to promote. The more ready you can be for this moment, the earlier you will succeed.

When is it time to leave your job?

One of the most common questions I get as an "experienced" executive is when it is time to leave a job. If you have found a position where you have passion for the mission of the agency and for your personal accountabilities, it's hard to decide to leave. If something comes along that presents even more exciting opportunity, that can make it easy, and if you love your job, likely more opportunities will present themselves. But as you get closer to the top of the pyramid, there are fewer opportunities. So, what should be your cues for it being time to move on, even if the next opportunity is not obvious?

You may wonder why should you move on at all. You are successful at your job and it may not even be clear who could do the job as well as you. Well, in fact even when you are successfully accomplishing the job, you might be hurting your agency in the long run and not serving the public well. Here are some ways to tell:

Do you have the fire-in-the-belly mentality for making things better? Most people when they enter a job see lots of things that need to be fixed, or at least could be done better. But if you have been there for a while, suggestions that things could be improved have a tendency to land differently. It begins to feel like personal criticism. You have been in charge for a period of time and if things are not running smoothly, then maybe it is time to acknowledge your accountability. Are you ready to try a new approach?

Or maybe things are going well, but you are feeling stale. Are you still seeking out new ideas and continuous improvement? Do you have the patience to hear people out without assuming you have heard it all before? You may have heard most of it before, but the person delivering the message may have evolved their thinking in some large or small way that creates an opportunity to find a solution. The plethora of information available today makes the need to remain open to old arguments that have fresh characteristics more prevalent than in previous decades. If you think you have heard it all, you are wrong, and it is time to move to another place where everything seems new to you.

Leave while your stakeholders and employees are still willing to applaud. You have likely put a lot of yourself into the job. You deserve to be acknowledged for that effort. Go when people still believe you have something left, although you can feel the passion slipping.

Leave when you believe you are an expert on everything and there is little left to learn. If this is the case, you have become an old fogey that few people want to be around. Leaving does not mean leaving public service. It means leaving the job you are in. It's time to regenerate yourself. It's hard to make this decision when where you are is comfortable. But you need to do it for yourself and for the organization you love.

It's also time to recognize your job is to assure that the public gets the best possible public service. In the short term, that may mean you staying in your job, but not in the long term, because someone else will bring enthusiasm and creativity that are as important as the job skills to successfully provide public service.

After you leave

Be prepared for the likelihood that after you leave your successor will find ways to make things better. When you leave the initial reaction will likely be that you are irreplaceable. There will be 'fans' who cannot imagine a different kind of leadership than what you provided. Don't believe it. Yes, occasionally a strong performer is replaced by a weak or unethical leader. But that's rare. More common is everyone has strengths and weaknesses. Leaders build organizations in their mold. Your organization reflects your strengths and weaknesses.

A new leader will bring their own strengths and weaknesses. They will have opportunities to course correct for your weaknesses. Be open and encouraging that new leadership will create opportunities for organizational growth. Because growth requires change and change is hard, a new leader will face resistance. Make it easier for them. Acknowledge that any leader will bring strengths, creating opportunities for the organization to get better.

One other part of leaving is hard. There is the old joke about leaving three envelopes behind for your successor to open when things get tough. The first envelope contains the message: *blame your predecessor*. The fact is nearly everyone does this. Nobody leaves a job without leaving problems behind, whether they know it or not. It may be a mistake, or it may be the problem was not adequately mature to understand or take action. These are particularly difficult from the outside to address because you no longer have access to information or authority to effectively understand and manage the challenge.

When I left BPA, for example, within a short time there was an internal operations issue identified that I had not recognized as significant, and hence, had not adequately addressed. Or it may not have matured to the point of executive action. Overall, one of my bigger weaknesses was lack of focus on internal business operations. I preferred the external policy focus.

When the problem surfaced after I left, I wanted to dig in to understand and offer advice, but that option was not available to someone officially outside the government. Ultimately, I learned my only choice was to speak my understanding of the truth, knowing that it was incomplete. I also had to act consistent with my values to take accountability, because the problem occurred on my watch. But that was difficult, since accepting accountability usually translates to taking responsibility to fix the problem, something I had no ability to do.

I don't believe I have yet adequately reconciled how to best handle a situation like this. Nevertheless, it will happen for many leaders upon leaving a high-visibility government position.

I was once Somebody

After you leave a significant role, all of sudden you are not as smart, not as funny, not as likely to be invited. In fact, the role of *I was once Somebody* is difficult for everyone. I was fortunate that a colleague of mine gave me the book, *The President's Club*, which chronicles how former US Presidents have defined roles for themselves and advised their successors. There is no one model, but every President appears to have thought they had more to offer than their successors did. Most importantly, they have found ways to make useful public service contributions after leaving leadership. These kind of lessons are helpful preparation for the blow to the ego that comes with not having as much relevance, but on the other hand not being irrelevant.

Conclusion

Learning on the job is hard for the incumbent, but even more so for employees. It also represents a loss of organizational effectiveness while the learning is taking place. Make the transition to new leadership easier by being prepared.

Similarly, do what is best for the organization by picking a time to leave that is months or years too early, rather than five minutes too late. And expect that leaders who follow you will forge their own way and make things better than you left them.

14

Live for Your Epitaph

Only a life lived for others is a life worthwhile.

—Albert Einstein

The best advice I have saved for last. Over the course of my career, I have worked with many professionals, and consulted many books on the subject of leadership. When working in the public sector, ultimately there is one rule unlikely to ever steer you wrong: decision-making should be focused on a long-term perspective.

With a long-range view on issues, the big questions help guide you as a leader: How would you want the decisions you are making today to be judged at the end of your life? How would you want your epitaph to read?

KEY TAKEAWAY

Live your professional and personal life by testing your decisions against a standard of how you would like people to talk about you at the end of your life. Doing so will lead to making decisions that best serve the public interest, as well as higher personal satisfaction.

How will history view your decisions?

If you consider every decision from the perspective that your actions and decisions will be reviewed by historians, it leads one toward operating on a higher plane. Make decisions with a focus on what you want to be remembered for, both from policy and conduct perspectives.

"Choose not just to be a public servant, but to embrace and celebrate public service."

What important policies were you able to contribute to that made the world a better place? What policy processes were you able to manage that led to greater public support, and therefore, policy longevity?

Choosing to live for how an objective third party would write about your life pushes one toward a public interest, rather than self-interest. Live how you want your epitaph to be written. It's the most strategic decision you can make. It makes the right ethical choices obvious, both in your public and private life. It helps your decision-making process when what you want cannot be achieved in a way that is right.

There is great power in choosing to wear on one's sleeve the pursuit of serving the public interest. It leads toward making decisions that the people around you recognize as focused on service to others. People gravitate toward leaders who exhibit these traits.

Turning down bonuses

After the west coast energy crisis ended in 2001, there were years of fall-out that impacted the choices we could make because of the huge financial losses that had been incurred. In many ways, these years were at least equally as difficult as being amid the extraordinary high prices and struggles to keep the lights on. Consumers, businesses, and government agencies were paying much higher prices for electricity, affecting lives throughout the Pacific Northwest. Unfortunately, at the same time, we had a string of below-average water years, making our financial recovery more challenging due to reduced revenues from our system, primarily based on hydropower.

At the end of 2001, I was awarded a bonus by the Department of Energy. But I had already eliminated bonuses for our employees as a cost-saving measure. This was during a time when corporate CEOs around the country were getting large bonuses at the same time that they were laying off large numbers of employees. It seemed obvious to me that I needed to return the bonus. I also decided to let it be known, because we were trying to build credibility with our customers, who were contractually committed to buy our power, that we were serious about cutting costs. Although a small amount of BPA's revenue requirement, it had the potential for significant symbolism.

It turned out that this small action of turning down my bonus generated a substantial amount of media attention. So much so, that the following year when I was introduced to Andy Card, White House Chief of Staff, in a White House hallway during an impromptu tour, he brought it up. I didn't expect him to know me, or if he did, I was concerned that he would associate my name with the political difficulties created for the White House by the west coast energy crisis. Instead, he patted me on the shoulder and said, "Hey, you're the guy who gave back his bonus."

It had been hard to give back the money, but whatever I would have bought with it was never going to be worth what I gained in terms of a reputation for integrity. More importantly, it became an important memorable moment for our customers as we sought to build their trust. That particular action probably resonated with customers more than the millions of dollars of budget cuts we put in place.

Subsequently, I declined four other DOE bonuses totaling more than $70,000. While those were not publicized, if I had taken them, they well might have been undercutting our efforts at trust-building. It did not make my wife happy when I made those choices, because she was the one who had to compensate for me not being available for the regular family responsibilities, as my disruptive schedule often got in the way. The money would have helped, if nothing else as salve on the wounds of not being as present as I would have liked for our family. But I don't regret the decisions.

I don't mean to imply I was always altruistic. Once the agency got back to financial stability, I began to accept bonuses. But there was a period of time when the self-interest conflicted with what best served the public interest. I needed to get that right for the organization to succeed.

Conclusion

The importance of building trust in our public institutions is an incredibly important role we play as public-sector leaders. Reflecting on what we want to be remembered for helps guide us to good decisions for the long term.

EPILOGUE

While the acclaim for the important role of public service may not be what would be hoped for, the actions of public servants are critical to supporting and maintaining democracy. Through personal leadership and management systems, instilling pride that leads to motivation is the most important tool available to public sector leaders seeking to provide the high level of public service necessary for government to be successful. Leaders who believe they can foster bottom-up bipartisan solutions create greater trust in government. Government leaders who minimize controversy, creating more focus on producing effective services that benefit the public, increase trust.

If you feel a sense of pride in improving the quality of life and producing meaningful outcomes for your family, friends, and neighbors, then choose not to be just a public servant, but to embrace and celebrate inspired public service. The more you can embody this philosophy, the prouder and more satisfied you will be. It will also generate more respect from the public and your fellow public servants. Ultimately, it leads to greater personal satisfaction for a life well-led.

Acknowledgments

This book would not have been possible without the teams I had the honor of working with at the Bonneville Power Administration and Chelan Public Utility District. There are way too many to name because so many were committed to making the agencies successful. They displayed patience when I needed to learn, brought forward innovative management tools, and provided valuable feedback even at times when I was not ready to hear it. These are great organizations filled with people imbued with the public service ethic.

The opportunities in my career came about because people showed faith by selecting me for positions that, with hindsight, I wonder how they thought someone so raw could succeed. There are too many to name without risk of missing someone critical, so I will not try. But I hope to have the opportunity to thank each of you personally.

My career in public service would not have been possible without the inspired professors at Central Michigan University and the University of Oregon. At CMU, I learned how to take a plethora of information and turn it into a lead through my journalism courses and the art of listening to understand in my psychology classes. At the UO School of Community Service and Public Affairs (now the School of Public Policy and Management), I painstakingly learned there is a skill to public policy analysis while also making lifelong friends. The training provided by these two universities established a solid foundation for what has been a tremendously satisfying career.

I am grateful to Michael Milstein who edited an early version of this book. I'm also appreciative of Doug and Katie Pauly, as well as Bob Bugert, who inspired me and provided detailed comments. High praise goes to my editor, Bryan Tomasovich, who had the patience and strength to tell me I needed to substantially revise my first draft to create focus. Bryan is skilled at his craft.

I am also grateful to the many people whom I have met in the stakeholder community associated with the electric utility industry. I use the broad term of *stakeholders* because I've learned from consumer and investor-owned utility personnel, independent power producers, regulators, non-governmental organizations, and many others associated with our industry. The electric utility industry provides a public service, and I view everyone associated with our industry as public servants.

Finally, I want to thank the many members of the public who have taken their own time to show up, have their voices be heard, and helped me to be a better public servant. I have been amazed and impressed with the dedication and time members of the public are willing to put in to help make their communities a better place to live.

Democracy is at risk as trust in our government continues to decline. This book shows how to strategically and systemically advance a high-performance public service culture built on instilling meaning, purpose, and pride. The simple, yet incredibly powerful concept of bolstering organizational culture with inspired public service can be foundational to restoring trust in government, a pillar to reinforcing democracy.

Leaders sincerely focused on the power of public service can improve government performance and build grassroots solutions to achieve bipartisan outcomes. Built on real-world experience, Wright provides instructive and entertaining guidance for public sector leaders—and potential leaders—about how to overcome negative societal perceptions, lead with time-honored values and informed decisions, and more broadly, rebuild confidence in government.

With over 40 years of public service, *Steve Wright* has led federal and local organizations with thousands of employees and annual revenues exceeding $3.5 billion. Wright has been in the bright public spotlight through political and financial turmoil, while giving hundreds of speeches, making dozens of appearances before legislative committees and regulatory agencies, and attending over a thousand meetings with members of Congress. He has been recognized with the highest awards for lifetime service from the United States government for executive civil service leadership, the American Public Power Association, and the Alliance to Save Energy.